Date Due

TALES
of
NOAH and the ARK

*

*

TALES
of
NOAH and the ARK

retold for Jewish youth

by Rabbi Charles Wengrov

Illustrated by Zalman Kleinman

*

SHULSINGER BROTHERS
NEW YORK

© Copyright 1969 by Shulsinger Brothers, Inc.

Set in Linotype Times Roman 14 point (with
Century Schoolbook, Bulmer, and Foundry Times Roman).
Composed and printed at the Press of Shulsinger Brothers
21 East 4th Street / New York, NY 10003

All rights reserved. No part of this book may be reproduced
in any form without permission in writing from the publisher,
except by a reviewer, who may quote brief passages and
reproduce not more than one illustration in a review
to be printed in a magazine or newspaper.

Manufactured in the United States of America

contents

1	A Strange Child is Born	7
2	The Wisdom of Enoch	19
3	Enoch Explains	32
4	Noah Brings Blessings	39
5	The Evil Grows Worse	52
6	Final Warning	59
7	Noah Builds the Ark	68
8	Seven Last Days	81
9	The Flood	94
10	As the Ark Floated on	107
11	The Winged Messengers	116
12	Return to Land	125

1

A STRANGE CHILD IS BORN

The world was still young and fresh, for only nine generations had been on the earth since the Almighty created Adam, the first man. In a crude hut sheltered under great flowering trees, a little baby lay on its soft bedding. It would be of the earth's tenth generation.

Since the child had been born, a few hours before, the mother had been in a deep sleep. Now she woke, and took the infant in her arms to have a good look at it. And her eyes opened wide in wonder. She even felt a little frightened—for in her lifetime she had seen many babies, born to other women, but never one like this. "Lamech!" she called her husband. "Come here at once." And Lamech, still tingling with happiness because he now had a little son, entered the hut swiftly. "What is it, dearest wife?" he asked.

"Look at this baby," she cried. "Look at his skin." And Lamech also felt a bit frightened. For in those early generations, children were born with rather dark bodies; yet this child was all white and pink—as white as snow and pink as a rose. In the minds of both Lamech and his wife there was one question: why was their baby different?

"Perhaps it is nothing," said Lamech. "In a few days he may become dark like other infants. Let us wait and see."

"But look at this also," exclaimed his wife, as she showed him the baby's hands. To you or me, the hands would have looked fine, perfectly normal. But to the parents they were most strange. For until that time, since the generation of Adam, no one had five separate fingers on his hand; all the five were connected by skin and tissue. This little child was the very first to have five separate fingers on each hand. Now Lamech was frightened indeed, but he still tried to calm his wife. "Let us wait a few days and see," he told her. "Perhaps this too will change, and he will become like everyone else."

The few days passed; and then the little child was able to open its eyes. Early in the morning, before the sun's rays yet reached their crude hut, its lusty cries roused the young mother. She picked it up tenderly—and then she called out, "Lamech, Lamech, wake up. Look!" Her husband stirred himself from his sleep and sat up. "What is it?" he asked.

There was no need for his wife to answer, for he could see for himself: Whenever the baby opened its eyes, the hut filled with a lovely golden light, as though the sun were already shining in. No longer could Lamech believe that his infant son would become like all others. It was no use to wait and hope. This little child filled him with worry. Moving with speed, he rose and went off to the hut of Methuselah his father. If anyone could tell him why his infant son was so different and what it meant, it was his own father. For Methusaleh had learned wisdom and Divine knowledge from *his* father, Enoch.

Methusaleh was then almost 370 years old; but in those early generations, when the world was yet very young, fresh and pure, all people lived for many hundreds of years before they died. Methusaleh himself was to live another 600 years—so that now he was really yet a young man.

He was pleased to see his son, and greeted him warmly. "What brings you to visit me, my dear Lamech?" he asked. Lamech described his baby son. "So you see, dear father," he finished, "he hardly looks like a human child. Perhaps he resembles the children of angels in heaven. Tell me, father: what does it mean? And if you do not know yourself, I pray you: go and speak with Enoch your father, and learn the truth from him. He will surely know, since he no longer lives among us on earth, but among the angels. Please talk with him as soon as you can."

"Yes," said Methuselah thoughtfully. "My father Enoch will surely tell me what it all means—why so strange a son has been born to you. For since he was

9

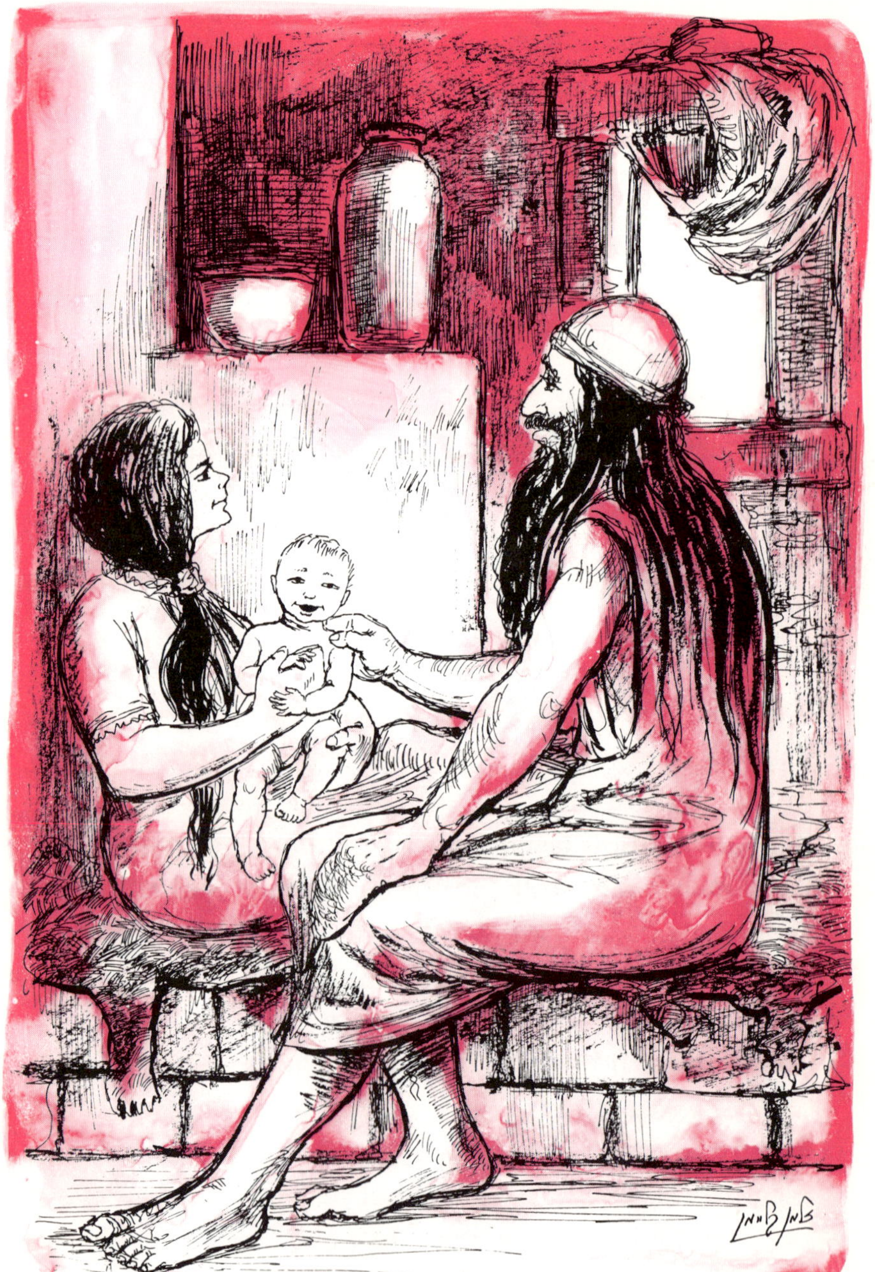

taken alive into heaven, there is nothing he does not know. Do you remember your grandfather?"

"Certainly," Lamech replied. "It is less than seventy years since he was taken up from earth." Methuselah and Lamech closed their eyes and saw again how Enoch had left them for the last time, almost seventy years before. "Did you ever hear," asked Methuselah, "how your grandfather became such a holy person?" No, Lamech replied; that he had never heard. "Then let me tell you about him," said Methuselah. And he continued:

All his years on earth, from the time he grew to manhood, Enoch had not lived like others. As he looked about, he saw people worshipping idols: they bowed down and prayed to little statues of wood and stone, because they believed that the statues were the images of gods—spirits that could help or hurt them. Thinking the idols would always protect them, they made weapons of iron and brass, and fought and robbed one another.

The trouble had already begun in the time of Adam's grandson Enosh, the son of Seth—in the third generation on earth. The root of the trouble was Adam's second son, Cain, whose very heart was evil. Long before Seth was born, Cain had killed his brother Abel in a fit of jealous rage. When the Almighty banished him, to keep wandering across the face of the earth, he did not change for the better. Wherever he went, he lived as a robber and a thief: when he wanted something that belonged to someone else, he either stole it secretly or seized it by brute force. As his children and grandchildren grew up, he taught them to be as evil as himself, until he soon became the leader of a whole group of outlaws, all lying and cheating, thieving and robbing.

The world lived on through centuries of time, as ever more people were born. The families and clans spread out further and further, to live in regions where no man had ever lived before. Some liked to be wandering shepherds, always moving on to new pastures with their bleating herds of sheep. Others found good pastureland and settled down to stay. Many more became farmers, tilling their soil and planting their crops, to grow their food from the land. And there were those who built up small cities and made thick walls around them, to keep enemies out. In those cities they set kings on their thrones, to rule over them.

Many were the skills they learned: to make lovely and useful things from wood and metal; to fashion handsome vases and bowls in baked clay; to play sweet music on new instruments.

So the people on earth lived then through their generations, when the world was young and human beings stayed alive for hundreds of years. But alas, the evil of Cain lived on also, in his children, grandchildren and descendants—for they were all as murderously wicked as their forefather. As their families came to live with the families descended from Seth, the people of Cain taught many of their neighbors to be as bad and vile as themselves.

Century followed century, and the wicked did not change for the better. And in the days of Jared, the great-grandson of Seth, matters grew far worse. It is told that a whole group of angels decided to leave heaven and live as people on earth, for they thought that as human beings they could have so much more pleasure. Though they knew they were sinning greatly, two hundred angels came down to the top of Mount Hermon and took a solemn oath to marry human wives and live as men. And the children born to them grew to be giants, yet more wicked than the families of Cain.

Enoch grew to manhood. He watched the world about him, and he knew that the evil things people did were dreadfully wrong. He saw Cain's descendant Tubal-cain discover how to sharpen iron and brass to a dangerously thin edge—and along came Azazel, a leader of the sinful angels who now lived as men on earth, and out of his dark secret knowledge he taught wicked persons everywhere to make armor and sharp weapons—knives, daggers, swords and spears. After that, wherever he looked, Enoch saw human beings murdering and robbing innocent neighbors, with no one to stop them.

Behind the cottage of Enoch's family stood a little hut that was always kept shut tight. Enoch's grandfather Kenan had lived there, and now, when he was living far away, many of his possessions remained in it. One day,

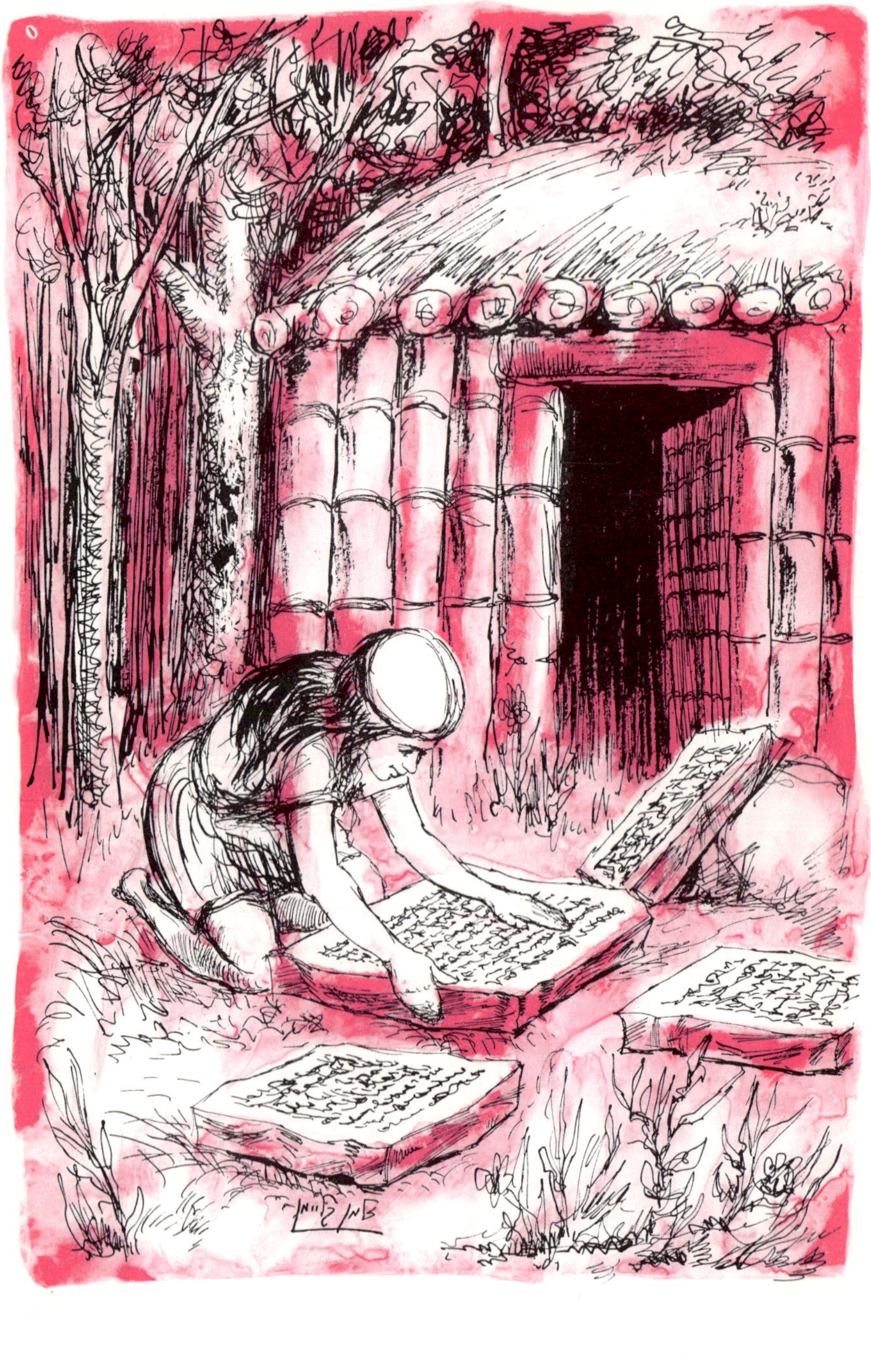

when he was almost grown, Enoch had nothing to do. Idly he worked open the door to his grandfather's hut and went in to rummage about. In a dark corner he noticed two stone tablets with writing on them. With every ounce of his strength he dragged them out into the light, and sat down to read them. And as he read, his heart beat faster.

It was his great-grandfather Kenan—he read—who had cut and chiseled these words into the stone surfaces, using a sharp iron point. The time would come, wrote Kenan, when the Creator of the world would bring a great flood to destroy every living creature on earth—because there was so much evil in the world. Kenan cut his words into the stone so that his warning would never be destroyed, but would remain for his family to read in later generations.

Suddenly Enoch remembered something his father had once told him: In the days of his great-grandfather Kenan, the waters of the great Mediterranean Ocean had risen and risen, until its ferocious waves had flooded a third of the earth. Clearly it was meant as a warning to the wicked people all around to change for the better. Yet no one paid any attention to that flood; they thought it a mere accident. And in Enoch's time, the people on earth were worse than ever.

Not for a moment did Enoch doubt whether he should take Kenan's warning seriously. He knew his great-grandfather was very wise in his knowledge of the

Almighty. For many years Kenan taught the people about him to give up their evil and to live as the Almighty wished. For a while the people about him listened, and they made him their king. But as Kenan grew old, the people drifted back into their wicked ways, and they stopped listening to him.

For hours Enoch sat looking at the stone tablets, thinking about this serious warning of his great-grandfather that reached him only now, so many years afterward. And Enoch slowly made up his mind. If all life on earth was to be destroyed some day, he wanted no part of the world's wickedness. He left his family and friends and went deep into a forest, where the thick trees kept human beings from ever coming. Entirely alone, he built a cottage to live in; and there he prayed long and earnestly day after day: "Almighty Creator, give the people on this earth a new heart—a pure heart, free of evil, that will love goodness and kindness and will hate wickedness. Teach the people on earth to worship You, to do only what is good in Your sight."

It was not long before Enoch knew that he was no longer alone: holy angels came from heaven to protect him and care for him. And one day he heard a heavenly voice: "Enoch, you who alone seek to serve Me, go to the angels that have sinned against Me. Go and call together all the angels who now live on earth as though they were men. And tell them that never will they find peace and rest—for never will I forgive them. Their evil sons are giants, yet all will die a violent death. They will turn to Me to pray and plead and beg, but I shall show them no mercy."

Enoch went back to the regions where people lived, and he called on Azazel their leader to bring before him all the two hundred angels who had left heaven to live as humans. Then he told them the Almighty's words. The angels trembled with fear, not knowing what to do. In desperation they turned to Enoch himself. "Since the Almighty has sent you to us," they said, "you are surely a very holy man. We beg you: pray for us. We no longer dare speak to the Almighty ourselves; we dare not even raise our eyes to heaven, so ashamed are we for our sins."

In his secret home deep in the forest, alone beneath the thick-leaved overspreading branches of the great trees, Enoch prayed for the sinful angels. Then he closed his eyes, and it seemed as though he were taken on a cloud, soaring gently into heaven, to be set down before the dazzling, radiant throne of the Almighty. And he heard the answer for the sinful fallen angels: "Go, and tell this to those who sent you here to plead for them: Angels should pray for men, not ask a man to pray for them. Why did you all run from the high heavens, where life is holy and never-ending, to have the unholy, troubled life on earth that ends in death? The sons born to you have grown into giants, and they live as evil spirits on the earth, murdering and robbing day after day. What good is it that you are sorry now for your great sin? You brought those vicious giants into the world, and they will continue to do evil—until I bring destruction and ruin upon the earth. So you will never find peace and rest, for I can never forgive you."

Enoch brought these stern words to the sorrowing Azazel and the fallen angels. Then he returned to his secret home in the forest; and for many years he was seen no more.

2

THE WISDOM OF ENOCH

The day came when this holy man heard an angel calling him, "Enoch, Enoch! Make yourself ready to leave your house. You will leave this secret place, for you are to remain hidden no longer. You now have the power to teach men; they will have to listen to you. Go, and teach them how they should live—what they should do and should not do—so that the Almighty may be pleased with them, as He is pleased with you."

Enoch returned to his old home, among his family. Every day he took his seat on a nearby platform of flat rock, and people felt drawn to stop and listen. At first only a few gathered to hear him; but as he taught with his heavenly words how a man should live in the ways of the Almighty, more and more came with each passing day. Until then none of them ever felt safe. Everyone lived in dread that some neighbor might come along at any moment to rob him, and perhaps to kill him. As they listened to Enoch, they realized how they could live in peace together, without fear—for all would vow to do no more crimes, obeying the Almighty's will.

So happy were the people to listen to Enoch's wonderful teachings, that they sent messengers far and wide to announce, "Whoever wants to hear the words of the Almighty; whoever wants to know how to live as a good person—come to Enoch, the Almighty's friend!"

If at first only a handful gathered before him, now they came in throngs, and they listened enrapt. Then, deeply grateful to Enoch, they made him their king, swearing to obey his teachings as faithfully as a man always obeyed a king's orders.

In time, even the sovereign rulers and governors of cities and provinces gathered to hear him. A hundred and thirty of them came, and not long afterward they too vowed to obey his teachings as if he were their king.

So Enoch saw peace and quiet come to the world about him, as the people on earth learned to live without stealing, robbing and killing. Once more, as in the blessed, peaceful years long ago, the men spent their time tending flocks of sheep in grassy pastures, working farmland to grow crops of food, or practicing their skills in the walled cities. The world was a good place again.

Only the giants, the sons of the sinful fallen angels, remained as vicious as ever. But Enoch taught the people to band together to defend themselves. As soon as a giant came along to harm someone, all the neighbors came running to pelt him with stones, until the giant fled for his life.

So passed two hundred and forty-three happy years

in the life of Enoch, as he continued to teach the Almighty's way to live. Then came a sad day, and it brought a great change in Enoch's life.

At the age of nine hundred and thirty years, Adam died. He was the very first man on earth, created by the Almighty Himself; and had he not sinned by eating the forbidden fruit, he would have lived forever in the Garden of Eden. But because he ate the forbidden fruit, the Almighty sentenced him that some day he must die. And now Adam's body lay lifeless at last.

By the wisdom that he had learned from the angels, Enoch knew what to do. Adam's body was very holy, since the Almighty had formed it Himself—and no living creature, animal or human, must be allowed to injure it or treat it badly. Tenderly, carefully, Enoch took the body and buried it in a double cave—a cave inside a cave, where no one ever knew to go, and where no animals ever wandered in.

Six days later, Eve died. As Adam was the first man on earth, his wife Eve was the first woman; she too had been created by the Almighty. Enoch's sorrow was now doubled, as he gently brought the aged body of Eve to rest near the remains of Adam in the double cave. As Enoch left, he saw the inner cave being sealed up; he knew this was the Almighty's doing. (In fact, the cave was to remain sealed for many generations, until the time came for a man named Abraham to bury his wife Sarah. He would know how holy the double cave was,

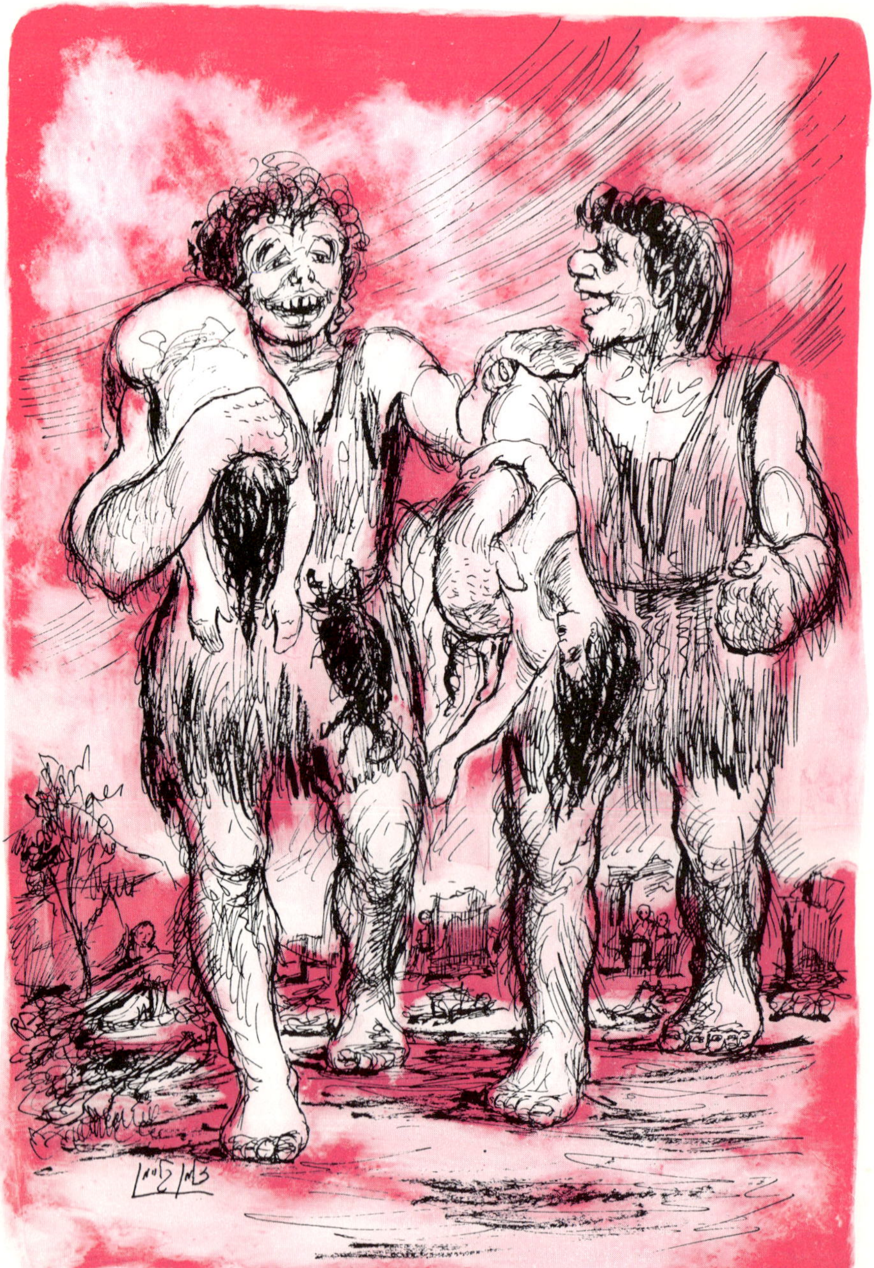

because the bodies of Adam and Eve were put to rest there, and he would insist on buying it from Ephron the Hittite. As more years passed by, Abraham too was buried there, next to Sarah; then Abraham's son Isaac and his wife Rebekah; and finally Isaac's son Jacob—the father of the Jewish people—and his wife Leah.)

Sadly Enoch realized that if Adam and Eve died, no one would live forever. No matter how long a person lived, in time he must leave his existence on earth. And there was so much more of the Almighty's holy wisdom that Enoch wanted to learn. Living as he did now among people, teaching the great throngs who came every day, he could learn nothing more than he already knew. Only in his secret home in the forest, far from every other human being, could the good angels return to teach him all he longed to learn. Yet how could he leave the people, when he was the only teacher and leader they had?

Enoch decided on a plan. After so many years of listening to him, the people of the earth would be able to get along without him for a few days at a time. Enoch went back to his hut in the forest, but he stayed there only three days. The fourth day, he returned to teach once more the great crowds who eagerly gathered to hear him. And this became his regular habit: three days he would remain apart, hidden in his forest home; and every fourth day he would be back to tell of the good and righteous life that the Almighty wanted people to live.

So many years went by, as Enoch returned to his fellow-men every fourth day. By then the people did not need him so often, and he began to return to them only one day a week. In time he came but once in two weeks, then once in three weeks, and finally no more than once a month.

Gladly would Enoch have continued to appear once a month before his fellow-men, for he had so much time left to worship the Almighty and learn His wisdom from the angels who were constantly with him. But he remembered Adam and Eve. Some day he would also have to leave the world; and before that time he had to teach his fellow-men to live good lives without him. So one day he began to return to them only once in two months; then once in three months, and later, once in four months, and so on—until he came before them only one day a year.

How the people on earth wished he would come more often—especially the kings and rulers who always came to hear him, for they always had serious questions to ask. They decided to find out where he stayed during the entire year, when he was away. The next time he appeared, for the one day of the year, they planned to follow him secretly when he left them, until they discovered his hidden home. Then they could visit him during the rest of the year. But when the day came and Enoch stood before them, the kings and rulers gave up their plan. For in the time that Enoch stayed in the forest, he had become as holy as the angels. His face shone with such pure radiance that they were afraid to look directly at him, fearing they would die. They no longer dared think of following him back to his secret home. Whatever they wanted to learn from him, they would have to ask him on this one day.

In sweet peace and serenity the years passed on. The day came once more when Enoch was to go to the people. His face shone more brightly and gloriously than ever; and as he appeared, a great, joyous shout rose up: "Long live the king! Long live the king!" For they knew that he alone was fit to rule as king over all their kings and governors. Enoch blessed them in the name of the Almighty, and as always, he began to tell of the wisdom he had learned.

Long and earnestly he spoke. Suddenly he paused, for an angel came to speak to him: "As you have become a king of men on earth, by the great things you have taught them, so has the Almighty decided to make you a king in heaven, among the angels. Prepare yourself, for soon you will be taken to heaven."

Enoch turned back to the people. "If any men have stayed away today," he said, "tell them to gather. Yet a few days more can I stay with you; then I am to be taken up to heaven. Let me teach you then, in these last few days, all that I can."

Three days later Enoch gave his last advice to the people on earth: "If you will live together in peace and

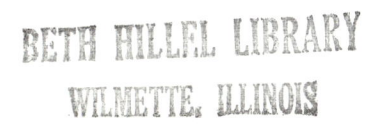

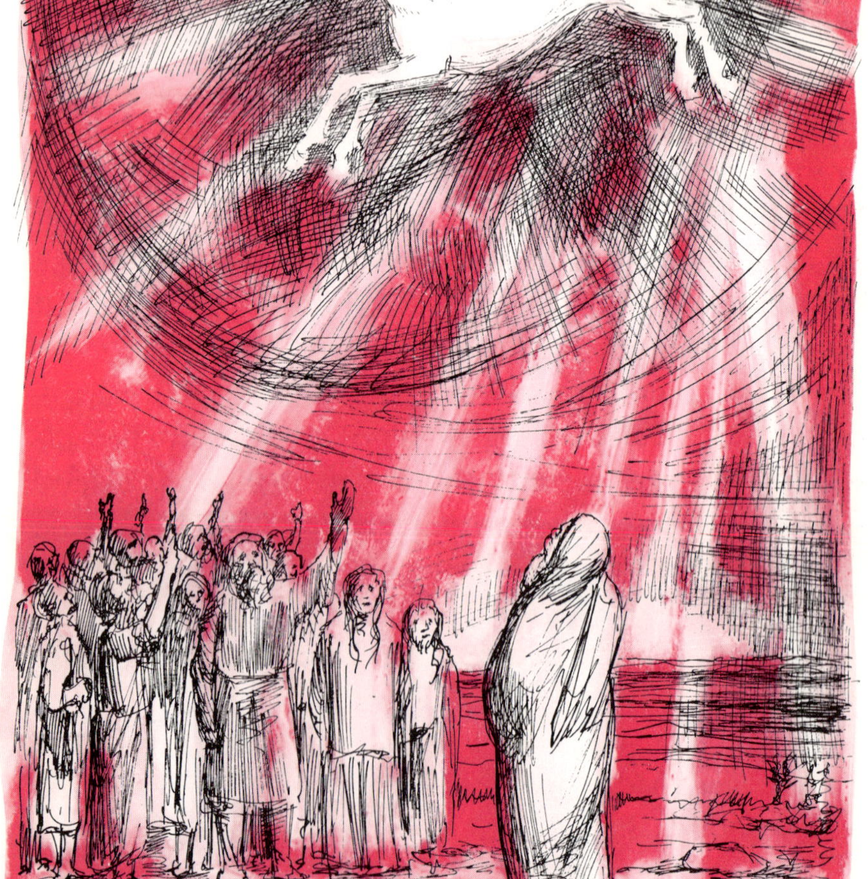

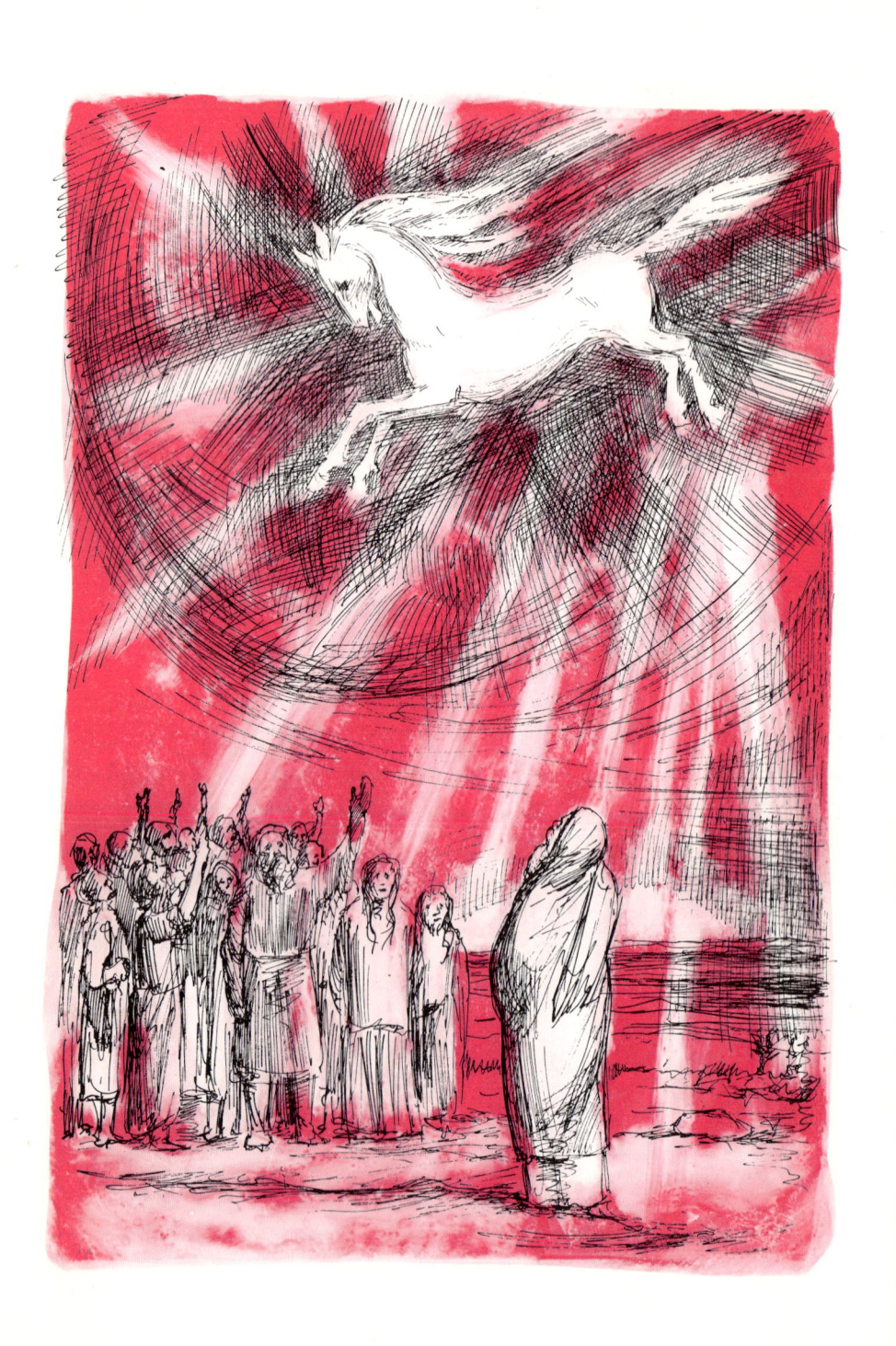

be kind to one another, the Almighty will be kind to you, and He will bless you with long and happy life." Then the people near to him exclaimed, "O Enoch, look: A horse comes down from the sky!"

"That steed must be for me," he replied. "The time has come for me to leave you for the last time." Before Enoch the horse came to a stop, and he mounted it. He blessed them, and the steed cantered away.

But the people could not bear to part from him. Eight hundred thousand followed him the entire day and night, never letting the horse and its rider out of their sight. The second day, however, Enoch turned around in his saddle and urged them, "Go back to your homes! If you follow me further, you will lose your lives!"

Most of the people listened to him and turned back. Yet some refused, crying, "We care not if we die; we will not leave you." So they followed him for another five days, paying no attention to his warnings. On the sixth day he said to them, "Go home now, I pray you. Tomorrow I shall go up to heaven, and whoever is near me will surely perish." Some turned back, but some remained. "As the Almighty lives," they cried, "only death will part us from you."

The seventh day came. It was the sixth day of the month of Sivan—Enoch's birthday. At the very same hour as he had been born, darkness fell, so that no one could see what was happening. And amid the darkness angels came, bringing a fiery chariot drawn by horses of fire, and they took Enoch upward. It is told that while he was yet far from the Almighty's throne of glory, the higher angels sensed that a human being was approaching. "O Master of all the worlds," they cried, "how can such a thing be? Shall a mortal man from earth come among *us,* to worship You in heaven?"

"My holy servants," came the Almighty's reply, "do you know that many years ago the people on earth left Me and forgot Me? They bowed down to idols of wood and stone, and did every kind of evil crime, driving Me far away from them. Enoch alone believed in Me. He learned My wisdom and taught the people on earth how I wish them to live. Let him now be a king among you."

The kings of the earth had left Enoch in good time to return to their homes. But they were curious to know what had become of the people who followed him to the very end. With their servants they went to find the men. As they approached the place where Enoch had been taken upward, they saw pure untrodden snow spread all about, like a smooth white blanket; and set in the snow were huge hailstones. With their axes they split open the hailstones; in each they found one of the men who had followed Enoch to the end. Not one was alive any more. But among them all, Enoch himself was not to be found. He was gone.

This was the story of Enoch, as his son Methuselah now related it to his own son Lamech.... For a while the two sat lost in thought. "It is hardly seventy years," said Methuselah sadly, "since he was taken into heaven—and how the world has changed. Do you remember? The very next day after his departure, the kings and rulers came to me and said: *You must take your father's place as our king of kings. You must teach us his wisdom, now that he is gone.*"

"I remember," said Lamech; "and you agreed."

"Of course," replied Methuselah. "As his eldest son, I knew the teachings of Enoch better than anyone else. In the years that he spent alone in the forest, he wrote down much that he had learnt from the angels; and he left his writings with me. . . . I was willing to let the people gather in great numbers, and I would speak to them as my father had done. And at first they came. . . . But they grew tired of living at peace and doing good. The throngs and crowds that came to hear me grew smaller all the time. More and more decided they would have so much excitement and pleasure if they became thieves and robbers again, like the evil giants who still roam the earth."

"Does anyone still come to learn Enoch's wisdom from you?" asked Lamech.

"No," was the reply. "Many years ago they stopped coming altogether to hear me. They are fools who do not see how foolish they are. For since they have turned back to evil, you know what has happened to their farms. Whatever they plant on their land, the weeds and thorns spring up everywhere, and time and again they go hungry because no food has grown on their farms. Yet they do not understand that the Almighty is punishing them in this way because they are so bad."

"It is far worse than you know," said Lamech. "There is a great famine now. Everywhere people are starving because they have grown no food on their fields. Your farm and mine must be the only ones that have not failed."

"We can thank Enoch for that," said Methuselah. "He taught us well, and you and I remain faithful to all we learned. This son of yours that was just born—we must make sure he too learns it as he grows up."

"Yes, father," answered Lamech. "But I wish I knew why he was born so strange—his skin all white and pink when everyone else is born with darker skin—and five separate fingers on each hand when everyone else has fingers only on the feet, for the hand is one piece of flesh. And why does our cottage fill with that lovely light whenever he opens his eyes? You *will* go and ask Enoch, won't you?" Methuselah nodded. Then Lamech asked, "Are you certain he will appear to you?"

At that Methuselah smiled. "I have already seen him several times, my son. He always comes when there is something I must ask him. He no longer has a body of flesh and blood up there in heaven, but a body of fire. His eyes are like torches, and his hair is one great blaze. He wears a magnificent robe, adorned with every kind of precious gem, that the Almighty Himself gave him; and on his head he wears a crown that gleams with forty-nine jewels. For a seat he has a throne beside the gates to the seventh palace in heaven. Nor is he called Enoch any more. Now his name is Metatron, and he is one of the most important angels in heaven."

Lamech felt calmer already about his strange infant son; he was certain that he would know soon what it all meant. "Once you have spoken to him," he asked his father Methuselah, "please come and tell me what he said." Old Methuselah nodded, and Lamech returned home in cheerful mood.

3

ENOCH EXPLAINS

Whenever Methuselah went to speak to Enoch his father (or the angel Metatron, as he was now called) it seemed to him that he was walking to the very ends of the earth. He left far behind the last traces of the cottages and huts where people lived, and continued walking for six days across desolate stretches of land, where no human or animal ever set foot. For he had to reach the very spot where the horses and chariot of fire had come to take his father soaring upward.

As he walked on through the lonely days, Methuselah thought of the last time he had come walking this way.

The people of the world around him had begun to stay away on the days that he taught the wisdom of his father. For a long while only the families that were descended from Cain stayed away. They inherited the wickedness of their forefather Cain, and they made their homes in the very field of Damascus where he had murdered his brother Abel. Once Enoch was gone, with his commanding voice that no one thought to disobey, it seemed only natural for them to return to sin and crime. They took the evil giants as their leaders, and formed bands of outlaws. And no one was safe from their terrible power.

On the mountains near the Garden of Eden lived all the families that grew from Adam's third son, Seth. Since their forefather had never been wicked, neither were they. They had no wish to forget the wonderful teachings of Enoch. As they had come faithfully to hear him, so they kept coming to listen to Methuselah. And they remained peaceful and kind.

Now, however, their lives were in constant danger. Almost every day the people of Cain appeared as the outlaws they had become, with the fearful giants at their head—and they raided, attacked and robbed whomever they pleased. Desperately the people of Seth turned to Methuselah, who lived among them (being also descended from Seth) and they begged him to help.

Methuselah still remembered how he had walked then to the same place that he was approaching now, to ask his father what to do. At the very spot where Enoch had been taken from earth, he built an altar for sacrifices, and he began to pray. For the last three days he had fasted, so that his prayer should be answered. Suddenly the altar shook violently, and from nowhere a short sword leaped into his hand. Then he saw his father before him, not as the Enoch he remembered, but as the

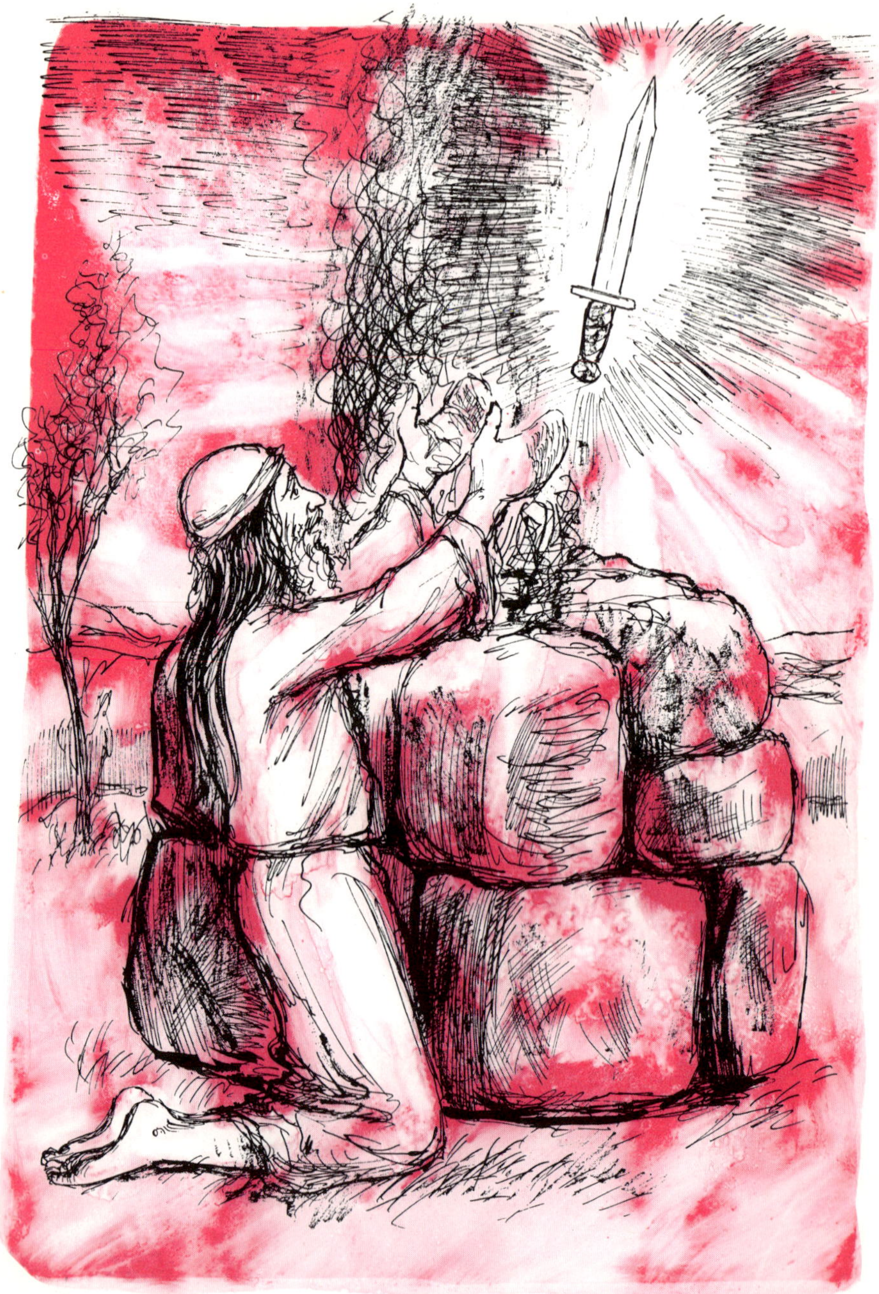

fiery angel Metatron. His father told him to inscribe on the sword the most holy name of the Almighty.

This Methuselah did; and when he returned to the people of Seth, there was no longer any reason for fear. From then on, whenever a band of outlaws appeared, led by a giant, Methuselah took the sword and went to meet them. Most fled in terror at the sight of that piece of gleaming metal; as for those who did not flee, the sword seemed to move of itself, dragging Methuselah along with it, and it cut and slashed the remaining bandits right and left. No one, nothing could stop it. So the people of Seth could live in peace once more, faithful to all they learned from Methuselah.

But alas, thought Methuselah, as he now walked on resolutely through the lonely, silent stretches of land —all that was a good many years ago. How different everything was now. For in time, young men of the people of Seth married girls from the families of Cain, while young men of the Cain families married girls from the people of Seth. And one day there were no longer two separate groups of people in the world about Methuselah, one good and one bad. All were bad. As in the years before Enoch, all now stole and robbed, maimed and killed—all, except Methuselah and his son Lamech, and their families.

Methuselah knew that Lamech and he still had nothing to fear. The sword on his wall would always protect them.

He walked on silently till he reached his destination—the very place where Enoch had left the earth.

At the altar Methuselah prayed silently. He never saw his father approaching; yet suddenly the angelic figure was there, in all his flaming glory. And Methuselah asked why so strange a child was born to Lamech.

"He looks strange," said the angelic figure, "because the Almighty has blessed him more than anyone else on earth. Therefore is his skin so fair, and his eyes fill the room with wondrous light. Even now, as a mere infant, he will bring blessings upon the earth; wait and see. But the greatest favor of the Almighty will come to him a full six hundred years years from now, when he will be the father of three grown sons. Then the Almighty's patience will end with the people on earth. For by that time the people will be so completely bad, so utterly wicked, that they will be unable to change for the good any more. The Almighty shall bring a great destruction then upon the earth: For one whole year a mighty flood will cover the earth with its raging torrents of water, until none is left alive. So shall the earth be cleansed of all the wicked, ugly things that the people do." Enoch paused; and Methuselah kept his eyes to the ground, fearing to look at his father as the fiery angel Metatron.

"However," said his awe-inspiring father, "this grandson of yours (the son of Lamech) will be a good man in the sight of the Almighty. And though the terrible flood will destroy all who live on earth, this son of Lamech and his wife will be saved, together with his three sons and their wives. For this reason was he born so fair—for he shall always be fair and good in the eyes of the Almighty. And his eyes fill the hut with light because he shall live by the light of the great wisdom that I have taught you. You alone will teach him, and he will pass on this radiant knowledge to his children after him."

It was another moment or two before Enoch (as the fiery angel) continued once more: "Lamech wonders and worries why his son has five fingers on each hand, like no other human being on earth. With such hands he will be more skilled than any man before him. He will take to farming, and the new tools his hands will make shall bring new, wonderful blessings to the earth.

"Now," said Enoch after another moment, "by what name will you call Lamech's child?"

"Since you speak of the blessings he will bring to the earth," replied Methuselah, "I think to give him the word *noah* for a name—for it means pleasing, giving pleasure—and he will bring joy and comfort to our earth, that is so accursed and burdened with evil."

"Good," said Enoch. "Noah is indeed the right name for him, as it also means to remain at rest. And he alone will remain, with his family, to rest on the earth when the mighty flood will have done its work to make the world pure once more. But let me warn you: Only you are to know this true name of his, which Heaven has already given him. Let not even his mother and father know it, until the child is grown and has learned to live with your wisdom and religious devotion. For if even his parents learn his real name, others will learn it too; and they will realize how precious, important and holy the little boy is. They will sense that he alone will be fit to be saved when the time comes for all on earth to die. Then men of evil will do everything in their power to end this child's life. For if they can remove little Noah from the world, the Almighty will be unable to bring the great flood upon the earth, and the men of evil will then be safe. There must be at least one good, religious person on earth who can remain alive through the flood, so that afterward a new human race can arise from him." Again Methuselah nodded in understanding.

"Then bear in mind," his angelic father ended, "that people will try to harm the child only if they know his true name. Tell it to no one until he is grown and becomes a man. Then his own goodness will protect him."

In the twinkling of an eye the blazing radiance of flaming fire was gone, for Enoch had vanished from sight. Methuselah trudged back the way he had come, lost in thought. All his father had told him rang crystal-clear in his mind. He would be able to repeat everything to his son Lamech word for word—everything, except the part about Noah being the child's true name, already given him in heaven. That Methuselah would keep entirely to himself for many years.

4

NOAH BRINGS BLESSINGS

Lamech listened eagerly to all Methuselah told him; and a great beaming smile wreathed his face. "Dear father," he exclaimed, "how happy your words have made me. I thank the Almighty with all my heart. . . . But now, what shall we name the child?"

"Perhaps," said Methuselah softly, "we can call him by the word *m'naḥem,* for it means a comforter, and he is sure to bring comfort and good cheer to our troubled, distressed earth. And if the people living on earth should only start to change for the better, he will bring them great comfort indeed." So it was that Lamech gave his son the name Menaḥem, saying, "This one shall bring us comfort and rest from our labor and the toil of our hands [to draw our food] from this earth which the Lord has cursed" (Genesis 5:29). And by the name Menaḥem everyone called him, while Methuselah kept his secret.

Enoch had promised that even now, as a tiny infant old but a week or two, he would bring blessings upon the earth. And his words came true.

When people of the world first began to worship idols of wood and stone, in the third generation since Adam was created, the ocean had come pouring and tearing past the shore in great waves, to flood a large part of the earth. For so the Almighty wanted to show the men on earth how wrong they were. Now, for months before Noah was born, the ocean was pouring again over the land twice a day, bringing serious floods every morning and evening. For the people in the world had turned evil, and again the Almighty sent them a warning, that they might give up their wickedness. Now that Noah was born, the floods stopped for his sake, and the seas stayed within their proper boundaries. For the word *noaḥ* also means "resting"; so the turbulent seas came to rest from their upheavals.

Soon people began to build their homes near the seashore once more, unafraid. Then everywhere another wonderful change happened.

When Adam sinned in the Garden of Eden by eating the forbidden fruit, the Almighty told him that as part of the punishment, "cursed will the ground be because of you. All the days of your life you shall get your food from it only with toil; it will grow thorns and thistles for you [instead of food], until you will have to eat the grass of the field" (Genesis 3:17-18).

Once Adam was driven out of Eden, he began to farm the soil, and he found that the Almighty's words were only too true. Day after day he struggled to pull out the worthless weeds, the sharp thorns and thistles that grew rapidly on his soil instead of the seeds he planted. But at last he managed to get enough of the weeds out so that the crops, such as wheat and corn, could grow.

The children of Adam, and the later generations, had to toil and struggle in their farming just like Adam. Then people everywhere began to make idols, statues of wood and stone to worship, for they believed that in the idols they saw little gods who had power in heaven. And a strange thing happened on their farms: If they planted wheat, thorns grew instead; if they planted barley, thistles came up. Whatever food crop they expected to get, they were sadly mistaken, for worthless weeds were all that grew.

It was the Almighty's way of trying to tell them that they were just as mistaken about the idols they worshipped. Even as the soil no longer gave them what they needed, so would they never get what they wanted from the little gods in whom they believed. But the people could not or would not understand, and the earth remained cursed in this way too. So it was that in the years before Noah's birth, famine came. Try as they would, the farmers could get nothing from their land but thistles and thorns. And mankind began to starve.

Not since the early days of Adam had such hunger come upon the world. When Adam was first driven out from the Garden of Eden, it took him a long while to

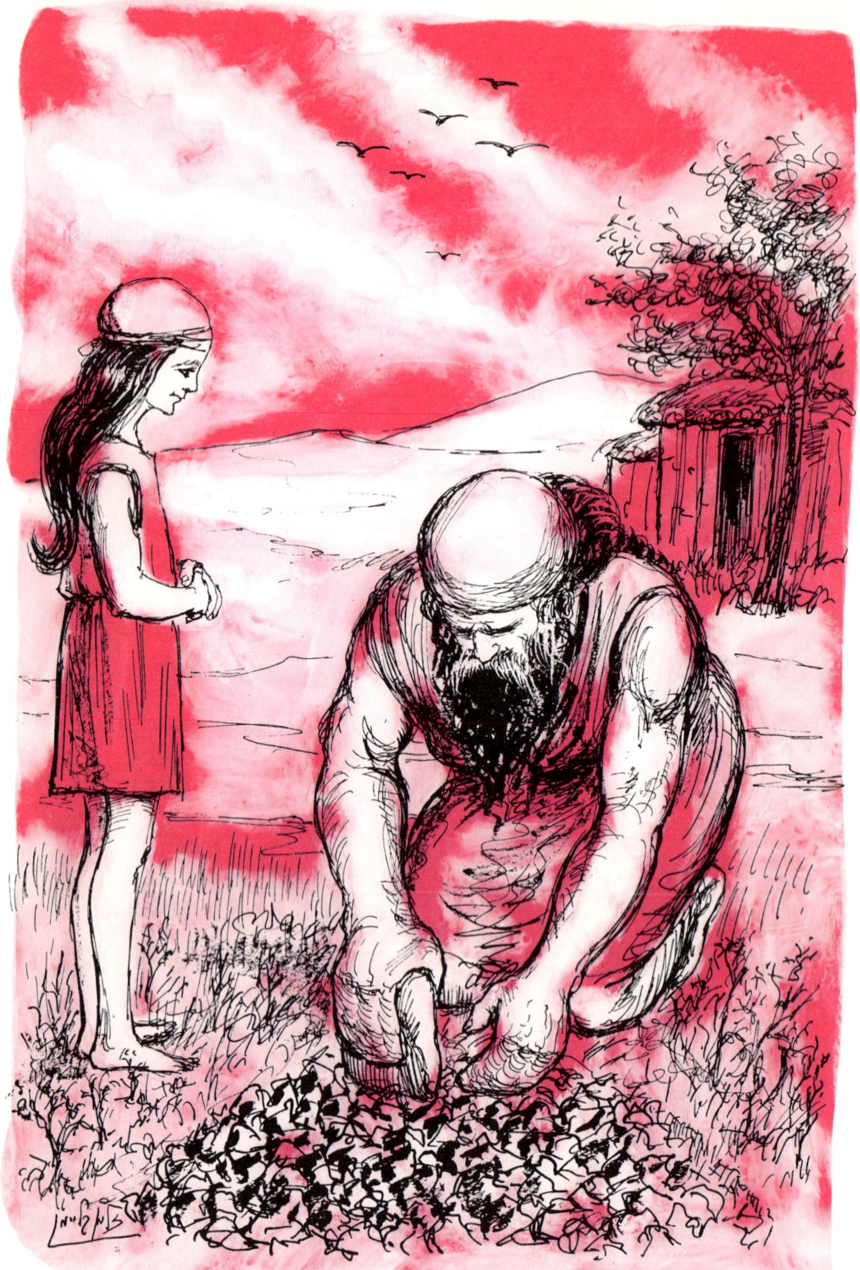

learn how to farm his land properly—to plow the soil, plant the seeds, water the earth, remove the weeds, and so on. Then he had to wait until his crops reached their full growth and were ready to be harvested. In all that time his family and he suffered the first famine in the history of man. They often starved, and had to live on "the grass of the field"—whatever leafy vegetables they could find that grew wild, by themselves.

In the years before Noah was born, the evil deeds of the people brought on the second famine in the history of the world. Once more people on earth had to look for "the grass of the field" and wild berries and roots that they could eat. But instead of being sorry for their evil ways and changing for the better, the people became worse. If anyone thought his neighbor had any food, he went at once to try to steal it or take it away by force. Each was ready to slay his neighbor for some food, so driven by hunger were they.

With the birth of Noah, the famine vanished as suddenly as it had come. For the earth no longer "made mistakes": From then on, a farmer got the crop that he planted, whether it was wheat or oats or whatever. The troublesome weeds, thorns and thistles disappeared. For *noah* means "rest," and as Noah came into the world, he brought the earth rest and peace from the curses and troubles that had befallen it ever since the Almighty told Adam in the Garden of Eden what his fate would be.

So tranquillity and rest came not only to the earth

but also to its farmers. They found it easier than ever to grow food on their land, and they were happy.

With the serenity of a flowing river the years passed, as Noah grew from infancy to boyhood. In time, as he grew older, Noah stopped his romping and playing, and he took to watching Lamech, his father, at work on the farm. He was eager to learn what his father did, and why, to make the earth grow food for them. For with all his heart he yearned to help his father in the long, hard work.

It was the season of the year to plow the soil—to turn the earth over, piece by piece, and break it up into loose particles, so that later the seeds could be planted in it. Noah watched his father squatting on the ground and using nothing but his hands on the soil around him. When he finished one part, Lamech moved on to squat again or kneel on the ground, to plow up the next part with his hands.

"Father," asked the boy, "why do you use your bare hands? Does it not make your hands ache?"

"This is how all farmers plow the land," answered Lamech with a deep sigh (for he was indeed bone-weary of this hard work). "This is how we make it ready for planting the seeds. Otherwise no crops could grow in the earth."

"But, father," said Noah, "why can you not make some tool of hard iron that will break up the earth for you? Surely it would be easier for you then. You could even tie the tool to some strong animal, perhaps an ox or a cow, and make the animal pull it through the soil."

Lamech smiled, pleased that his son was so bright. "There were people who thought of this long ago," he said. "They made such tools of iron, and called them plows—and the plows looked good. But no one could make them work in the soil. They always twisted and turned and jumped aside—as though the earth itself fought them off. You know that when Adam sinned in the Garden of Eden, the Almighty told him the earth would be cursed because of him. I think this is all part of the same curse. Why, we cannot even plant our seeds in furrows, in straight rows on our farms. The earth itself seems to force us to plant them in all sorts of crooked, twisting rows. As for getting an ox or a cow to help in our work, many have tried that too—and the animals would not obey. When Adam lived in Eden, he was master of every animal. Oxen and cows would do his bidding; donkeys would carry his loads; and he could ride on horses. But since he sinned, man has lost control of those animals, and they will do nothing for us."

Noah said nothing, but merely watched as his father continued to work. His mind, though, was busy with thoughts. He had known for some time that he alone had separate fingers on his hands. Everyone else had hands of one piece (that resembled mittens). With his hands he should be able to do things far better than

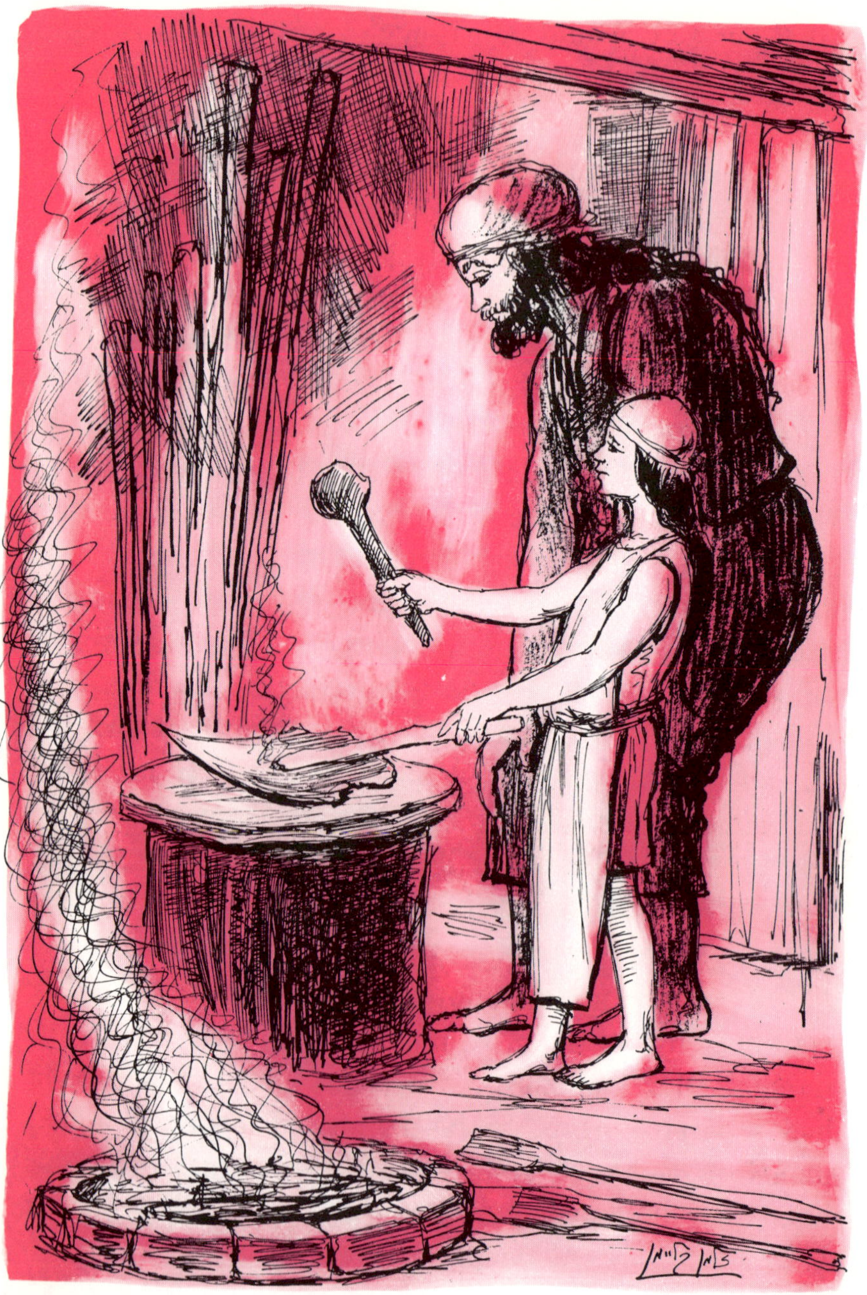

anyone else. Perhaps he could make a really good tool, that would work well in the soil.

As his father moved on in the field under the bright afternoon sun, Noah slipped away and went to a neighbor who was a blacksmith. For many months Noah had come often to watch this man also at work, and by now he knew everything the blacksmith did. In fact, lately he had begun to help the blacksmith, for with his fingers there was much he could do easily.

That afternoon, however, Noah did not come to watch or help; he had his own purpose in mind. Slowly he asked the blacksmith if he might try to make something for himself; and when the man agreed, he set to work softening pieces of iron in the fire and forming them into certain shapes. He worked steadily, in silence, until the setting sun made the light start to fade. Then he knew he had to return home. But the next morning he was back; and again he worked away steadily, through all the day. It was another few days before he was finished; then he held up what he had made.

The blacksmith was curious. "Whatever in the world is that?" he wanted to know.

"I hope it will be a plow," said the boy Noah, "a tool to break up the soil, so that my father will not have to do it by hand. I wonder if there is some land nearby where I could try it out."

"There certainly is," replied the blacksmith. "Here in the back is a great stretch of ground that belongs to me. But I never use it. Go ahead and do whatever you wish over there."

"I certainly thank you," said Noah. "But if you please, there is something else I need. Do you know anyone who might lend me a cow?"

"Now why would you need a cow?" asked the curious blacksmith.

"Well, if you please, I want the animal to pull my plow through the soil. I would get all tired out at once if I pushed it myself."

A smile came to the blacksmith's face. "You certainly have ideas," he said. "There is a neighbor of mine who keeps a few cows, and I am sure he will let you take one for the day. Go straight down this road, and you will soon reach his farm. Tell him that I sent you. But mind you, take good care of that cow and see that it gets enough grass to eat."

With a happy shout, the boy ran off.

Not long afterward Noah was back, leading a large brown and white cow by a leather thong or strap tied loosely about its neck. On the land behind the blacksmith's shop he attached his new instrument to the cow with a few more leather thongs. Then he stuck the sharp blade of his plow into the ground, and he made the cow pull. Behind him stood the curious blacksmith, looking on. And both man and boy were astonished. For the cow obeyed the boy Noah—something most unusual in those times—and it willingly pulled hard, until the plow broke up the soil perfectly. "You have done something wonderful," shouted the blacksmith.

Noah picked up his new instrument and led the cow away as fast it would walk, heading directly back to his father's land. "Father, father," he cried as he caught sight of Lamech, "I made a plow, and it works!" Once more he attached it to the cow with leather thongs, and he plunged the sharp blade into the soil. Once more he led the cow to pull hard. And again it worked splendidly —this time to the amazement of his father. "Look at that," marveled Lamech; "how the cow obeys you when you lead it. And this plow is excellent. What a blessing it shall be for me in the hard work on the land. It is just as Enoch told Methuselah my father: This is why the Almighty gave you different, blessed hands."

Losing no time, Lamech bought an ox, and day after day he had it pull his son's new plow to break up the hard-packed soil. It was not long before his neighbors came to watch, hardly able to believe their eyes. Then off they went to the nearby blacksmith, one demanding more loudly than another, "Make me a plow like that one, at once!" With the boy Noah to help him, the blacksmith learned exactly how to make it, and then he worked without a stop for days without end, from sunrise to sunset, to turn out enough plows for all the farmers.

Further and further spread the news of the wonderful instrument that Noah invented. In one region after another, then in one land after another, farmers learned of it. And their blacksmiths had to discover how to make it, so they could turn out enough for all the farmers around them. And everywhere cows and oxen obeyed their masters and pulled the plows. Horses became gentle and let people ride them. Donkeys carried human beings and heavy loads. For Noah indeed brought blessings to mankind.

To the mind of the young boy came more thoughts and wonderful ideas. With his deft fingers he made a harrow, a frame with sharp iron teeth on it. After the plow made separate pieces of the packed soil, he had his father's ox pull the harrow through the ground. It broke the heavy clods and pieces of earth into fragments and dust, which the harrow left lying evenly on the field. This too his father would no longer have to do with his bare hands.

It did not take long for farmers everywhere to make harrows for themselves. As the months went by, Noah's skilled hands made a hoe to move and spread the loosened soil about. He made a sickle and a scythe, whose sharp blades could cut the full-grown crops at harvest time. He made a spade for digging up the soil, and many more things that would help a farmer.

Everywhere the people copied his wonderfully useful tools. And in time the curse of hard, back-breaking work was gone from farming—the curse that had come when Adam sinned in the Garden of Eden.

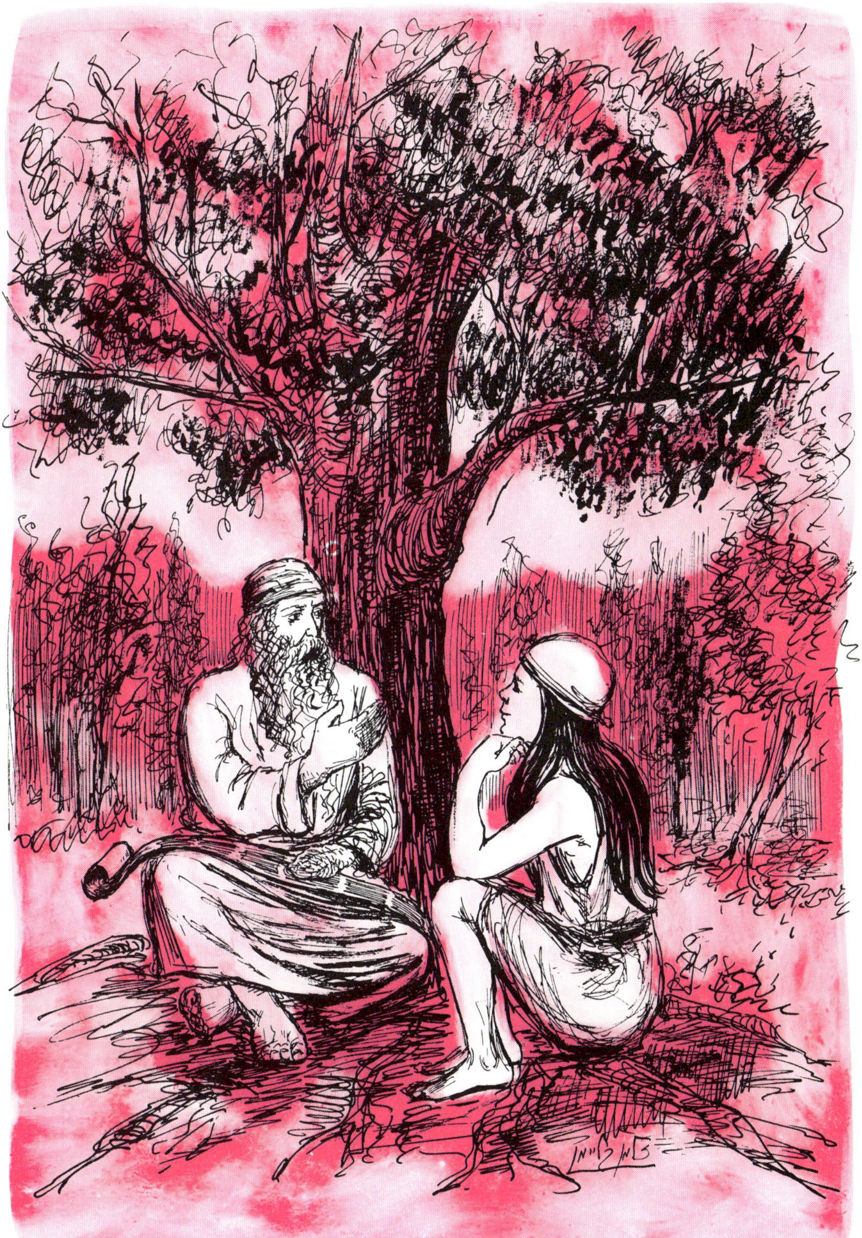

5

THE EVIL GROWS WORSE

The sun rose, and the sun set; so the days went by, and the weeks slipped away, and the years passed on. Noah grew taller as he began to approach the years of a man.

He began to study with Methuselah, to learn the wisdom of Enoch. Every afternoon they sat together, the grandfather who was now close to 400 years old, and the grandson who at thirty was not yet a man, since people lived then for hundreds of years. Under a fig tree they sat, as the leaves made dappled shadows in the sunlight; and they studied in soft voices the many pages of parchment that Enoch had written in his years of solitude in the forest.

In Noah's heart the wisdom of Enoch settled as level, clear and still as water in a vessel. All the wondrous ways of the Almighty that Enoch had taught and written now became a part of Noah's very being. Never would he forget what he learned from Methuselah under the softly moving leaves of the tree.

As Noah bcame a full man at last, Methuselah revealed to him that this was his real name, which Heaven itself had given him; it was not Menahem, as his father and everyone had always called him. He was free to use his real name the rest of his life: for now that he was grown and knew the holy teachings of his great-grandfather Enoch, no evil could harm him. So people forgot the name Menahem and came to know him only as Noah—this tall, fair young man who won the Almighty's favor because he followed faithfully the wondrous teachings of Enoch.

Like his father and grandfather before him, Noah became a farmer in earnest, working from sunrise to sunset to till the soil and harvest the food it grew. With his deft fingers, and with the various farm tools he had invented, Noah found his work easy—and the crops grew far better and richer on his land than on any other field. Year in and year out, when he cut and gathered his wheat, oats and barley, and vegetables and fruit, he had more than enough for himself and his parents.

"Father, said Noah one day, "you need not work any more. It is hard to do all the heavy tasks that a farm demands, and you are getting on in years. I raise more than enough food for you *and* for me."

"You speak as a good and loyal son," Lamech replied, "for it is a son's duty to support his father when the father grows old. But," added Lamech, smiling, "I am not yet aged. I am barely 300 years old, and more than half my life is still ahead of me. And even if you provide the food I need, I must still work my farm to support Methuselah *my* father. For that is *my* duty, as his son."

"You still have no need," insisted Noah, "to toil and struggle on your land. I can support both you and my grandfather Methuselah."

"What are you saying?" exclaimed Lamech. "Long ago, people asked Adam's first grandson if he would take care of his father in his older years, and he readily agreed, for his father had brought him into the world and taken care of him when he was a child. But then they asked the young man if he would also provide for Adam, and he refused. *What is that man to me?* he asked. *He never took care of me. It is enough that I provide for my father.* And ever since, this has been the rule of the world: a son takes care of his father in his old age, but of no one else. If a man grows so aged that his own son becomes too old to provide for him, he has to beg for food or starve to death."

Noah laughed: "What care I for such a rule of the world? It was my grandfather Methuselah himself who taught me that the Almighty has put us on this world to help and be kind to one another. I shall certainly give him too all he needs to live in comfort. But tell me: are then not other forefathers of mine still living? Methuselah's grandfather Jared . . . and *his* father, Mahalalel

". . . and then *his* father, Kenan . . . I think they are all alive."

"Yes," said Lamech. "I know where they live. Kenan and Mahalalel are *really* old."

"You must help me to arrange it," said Noah, "and I will make sure they get all the food they need as long as they live."

It is told that the Almighty noted what Noah said, and He was greatly pleased with the young man. "See what he plans to do," the Almighty told His ministering angels. "Do you know why I have let these early generations since Adam live for so many hundreds of years? I wanted people on earth to see their grandfathers and great-grandfathers alive and growing old. I wanted to know if they would have kindness and pity enough to care for the old ones in their own family. And not even the best of them has done so. Noah alone understands My wish and obeys it. I find only Noah so virtuous and good before Me in this generation."

Noah continued his farming, and as the earth grew crops aplenty for him, he generously shared everything with his father, his grandfather, and the three forebears who were still living.

The years passed by, and Noah reached the age of sixty, then seventy, and eighty. As human beings lived so long then, they took longer to reach manhood; between the ages of sixty and eighty a man would marry and begin to raise a family. Noah, however, refused to take a wife and raise a family. For he looked well at the world about him, and all that he saw only saddened his heart.

Since the tools he invented had made farming easy, many relatives of Lamech, his father, settled down on their land to till the soil and get their food honestly from their crops; and no more would they go stealing and robbing. But most of the world's people remained as evil as ever. They might spend their days as farmers too, or as shepherds, but they would still kill a neighbor readily to get something of his that they wanted. And the evil in the world grew steadily worse.

Noah watched the relatives of his father raising their children, and he sadly shook his head. The grown-ups turned honest and good; yet hardly any of their children became like them. As the young ones grew older, they found it more exciting to follow the evil ways of the rest of the world; and when the children were fully grown, many joined the bands of outlaws led by the wicked giants, eager for the "adventure" of plundering and robbing innocent people.

Filled with foreboding and worry, Noah decided it was best not to marry and raise a family. Why bring children into the world if they would almost certainly turn wicked like most of mankind? Wicked sons would only anger the Almighty. So Noah decided not to take a wife.

Time moved on, as Noah the farmer lived quietly through the months and the years. When he was 179 years old, his forefather Kenan died at the age of 910. As Noah became 234, Kenan's son Mahalalel died at the age of 895. And when Noah reached the age of 366, Mahalalel's son Jared (who was Methuselah's grandfather) died when he was 962 years old.

Through all these years Noah watched to see if the people about him would perhaps give up their wickedness. As far as he knew, no one changed for the better. They worshipped their idols, and stole and robbed as much as ever. Yet a remarkable change for the better came over the world. Farmland became so fertile and rich that in one season enough food grew for forty years. Never before had it been so easy for mothers to raise children: Like young horses or calves, newborn children could stand on their feet and walk only hours after they were born; and in a day or two they began to talk. As for the weather, it seemed to come from Paradise: winter and summer, the air was clear, warm and pleasant, as on the fairest day of spring. And the people of the world grew stronger and mightier than ever: They could go with giant strides to cover great distances in a day. Walking by a tall, mighty cedar tree, anyone could uproot it with one heave. And with their bare hands they could defeat any lion or tiger with ease.

Noah could not understand it. Why did the Almighty let the wicked live through these centuries with so much power, pleasure and ease? Why was everything so good for them? At last Enoch came to him in a dream, as the fiery angel Metatron, and he answered the question: "Do not be puzzled, dear grandchild of my son. The Almighty wants these bad men to know how wonderful life can be, both on earth and in the world of eternal life, if they will but obey the Almighty and become good. The time will come when people on earth will be given a stern warning: they must stop their wickedness and live as the Almighty wishes, or they will be destroyed. Perhaps they will heed the warning, now that they know what a pleasant world they can have."

But the life of ease and pleasure only made people more proud and evil than ever. They felt very sure, amid their comfort and power, that whatever they did, no harm could touch them. With muscles of iron and more food than they needed, they saw no reason to change for the better.

The evil of man simply continued to spread; when Noah reached the age of 480, there was more sin, cruelty and bloodshed on earth than ever before, since the time of creation. The Almighty's patience began to end.

6

FINAL WARNING

It was a day like any other day when Noah became 480 years old. The sun pleasantly warmed him, and the wind gently cooled him, as he plowed his field. Then, without warning, he heard words from the Almighty: "Noah . . . leave your plow and listen to Me." He stopped his work and stood humbly, with his head lowered. "Take Methuselah with you, and go with him to every part and corner of this world that lies about you. For I want you to warn the people on earth: Let them give up their evil ways, and I will give up My plan to bring destruction and death upon them. They have only 120 years left—no more. If they will not obey Me and turn away from all the dreadful things they do, then 120 years from now *I* shall do something dreadful, and no one will remain alive on earth."

"O mighty Creator and Ruler of the world," asked Noah softly, "if You must bring death and destruction, what will become of Lamech my father and the other good people?"

The Divine answer came: "Before I bring any punishment, I shall end the life of every decent, kindly person on earth, and bring them to live forever in the heavenly world of the spirit. The last one to be taken will be Methuselah, for he will live on earth longer than anyone else. You, however, shall remain on earth with your family, and you will live through it all—so that afterward you and your sons may begin a new race of human beings."

In silence Noah went to find Methuselah. He began to tell his old grandfather the words of the Almighty, but Methuselah stopped him. He too had heard this Divine message. The two set off together.

They went everywhere, day after day, trudging far and wide—beginning always at sunrise and not stopping till the light of the sky was gone. And everywhere the result was the same: people scoffed and laughed at them. "Who is this Almighty that spoke to you?" they sneered. "We worship our idols, and our gods will protect us. You say the Almighty is in heaven, and none can see Him. Then what can He do to us? Will He stop the heaven from sending us rain for our farmland?—What do we care? We can always get water for our land from the rivers and lakes and streams. Do you not know that we have to grow our crops only once in forty years, and we have enough food?"

Others jeered: "We have heard of this Almighty. It is said that He lives beyond seven heavens. Then how can He see what we are doing, when all those heavens block His view? And if he does not know what we are doing, then both of you are lying."

Finally, there were those who asked, "If He brings death to the whole world, how will the two of you be saved? Or does He mean to destroy you also, even though you have lived good lives?"

"The Almighty has promised to save my life," said Noah.

"And my life," said Methuselah, "will end naturally before He sends His great punishment."

Once more the people scoffed. "Then we have nothing to fear as long as you are alive," they shouted at Methuselah. "You look very hale and hearty to us. We will wait till your life is over, and then we will worry about your warning."

So it was that long after they set out from their homes, Noah and Methuselah returned to their homes, and they knew that all their heartfelt pleading words had fallen on deaf ears: Not one person had decided to change for the better. Let 120 years pass, and the great disaster was sure to come.

One evening Noah sat alone in his cottage, musing. He wondered what it would be like when he and his wife and sons were the only people alive on earth, as the Almighty had promised. And suddenly he realized that he had no wife and sons, because he had never married.

Then the Almighty's words could mean but one thing: he ought to marry without delay.

Soon afterward he became the husband of a fine, religious woman named Naamah, who had been born to Enoch in his last years on earth, shortly before he was taken to heaven alive. Not much older than Noah (as time was measured then), she had been raised by her vastly older brother Methuselah; and Noah could not have found a better wife. In the next few years she was to bear him three sons: Ham, Japheth and Shem. As they grew older, Noah realized that Shem was by far the best of the three. So he treated that one as his firstborn, and thought of his children as Shem, Ham and Japheth.

Hardly had the third son been born when Noah heard again the words of the Almighty: "The time is coming for Me to end all mortal life on earth—for the earth is filled with violence because of all who live on it, both man and beast. I promised to wait 120 years from the time that you and Methuselah spoke to the people. When this time ends, I will destroy them."

Noah was saddened to think of it. "O mighty Ruler of the world," he pleaded, "is there nothing else that can be done with them?"

The reply came: "Noah, you have seen kings among the people on this earth—how they sit in their palaces in the walled cities, to rule in honor and glory. Now, suppose a king built a palace and filled it with many servants and court-attendants, who could utter not a sound; yet every morning they would rise and greet him with great honor and good cheer, showing their respect and admiration by gesturing with their hands, bowing low from the waist, smiling, and so on. The king would surely be pleased; and he would think: *If these poor soundless creatures pay me such respect in affection, how much more would I be honored if I had people here who could speak!* Well, then: suppose that after a while the king brought in other servants and court-attendants, and these had the full power of speech; but instead of giving him any praise or honor, they seized control of the palace, crying, *This house is not the king's; it is ours, and we can do as we please here.* Think, Noah: would the king not have to drive them out? remove them completely?" There was no answer that Noah could give.

"When I created the world," continued the Almighty's reply, "the seas and oceans came into existence first; and their awesome waves and ferocious roar told of My majesty and grandeur. The mighty mountains are silent, but they too bear witness to My power. Now I have put human beings on earth who can see and think, understand and speak. How much more should they realize the power and glory of the One who made this world. How much more should they acknowledge Me and praise Me. Yet all they have ever said to Me is:

Do You stay in the heavens, for we want no part of You. This earth must belong to us!" Again Noah was silent, as he stood with bowed head.

"There is nothing else for Me to do," the words of the Almighty went on. "They must be removed from the earth. But I have promised that you and your family will live. As soon as your sons are grown, let them marry, that their wives may be saved with them. And this is what you must do beginning now, without delay: Make an ark for yourself, out of smoothed planks of gopher wood; make rooms and cabins in the ark, and cover it inside and out with a coat of pitch" (Genesis 6:14). Noah wanted to ask *why* he would need the ark; but he said nothing, knowing he must hear more. The Almighty's words continued:

"Now, this is how you are to make it: The length of the ark is to be 300 cubits, fifty cubits its width, and thirty its height. You shall make a great opening for the ark (Genesis 6:15-16), to hold a window that can be opened and shut; and put many sparkling diamonds and precious jewels there too, so that in the many days when the window must be kept locked, they will light the ark with the brilliance of daytime. The roof should not lie flat, but should slope upward from the two long sides, so that when you finish it at the very top, it will be only one cubit wide there. The door of the ark you shall set in its side; and you shall build it with three floors: a lower, a second, and a third deck" (Genesis 6:16).

At the same time that Noah heard this, a vision came before his eyes: He saw the little finger of a hand that was all a blazing flame—as it drew a picture in fire across the sky, to show him the ark he was to build. Then the Divine words came to him again:

"For I am going to bring a flood of waters upon the earth, to destroy under heaven every creature of flesh that has the breath of life in it. All that dwells on earth is to perish. But I shall keep My covenant, My solemn agreement that I make with you; and you shall go into the ark and be safe—you, and your sons, and your wife, and your sons' wives, with you" (Genesis 6:17-18).

"O mighty Ruler of the world," said Noah softly, "is it a flood, then, that will bring Your punishment? Yet that will destroy not only mankind but all animal life on earth as well. True, the people on earth have sinned dreadfully; but how have the animals sinned to deserve it?"

The reply came: "You have wisely lived apart from your fellow-men, to keep away from their wickedness; so you know not what they have done. Through the long years they have trained the creatures of the animal kingdom to fight and kill without purpose, either for food they do not need, or simply out of a lust for bloodshed. They have made the creatures of the field as wicked as themselves. Let the earth be cleansed of them too, that it may make a fresh start. Never fear, however: just as you and your family will take refuge in the ark, so will a few creatures of every species on earth, which have not learned man's evil. Of every living creature of flesh, you shall bring into the ark two of every sort, a pair—male and female—to keep them alive with you. Every kind of bird, every kind of beast, every kind of creeping insect and creature of the earth—two of each shall come in with you, for you to keep alive. And provide yourself with every sort of food that is eaten, and store it with you, so that it will be there for you and for them to eat" (Genesis 6:19-21).

Noah closed his eyes. In all his life he had never built anything more than a simple hut or cottage. How would he ever build a gigantic ark to house every kind of creature on earth? And the ark would have to be sturdy and well-made to withstand raging flood waters that would bring death to all.

Another thought made Noah worry yet more: How would he ever care for all the creatures that would be in the ark with him as long as the flood lasted? Where would he get enough food, where would he find enough strength, to make sure none went hungry?

"O mighty Ruler of the world," murmured Noah, his head yet bowed, "You have every power; there is nothing You cannot do, if You but wish it. Then surely You can keep us all alive—people and creatures—even without an ark. I recall how my great-grandfather Enoch was taken alive into heaven. Perhaps all of us could be kept safe in the same way until the flood is over, and then we can be returned to earth."

The Almighty's answer came at once: "You ask this because you fear it will be too difficult for you to build the ark, and you think you cannot care for all the earth's creatures in it. I do not lack for angels to help you. You will be given wisdom for your tasks, and you will know what to do. And whenever you find something beyond your strength, you will be helped."

Noah felt happier.

"But you wonder why I need the ark," the Almighty's answer continued, "and I shall tell you. You have spoken to the people of the world, yet they have not listened. Now I want them to see you building the ark. You will not build it near your home, hidden away from sight, but on a high plain, where all can watch. Perhaps when they see you working at it steadily, day after day, in preparation for the flood, they will believe at last that the flood is truly coming. Once they believe it, they may turn to Me and finally stop their evil—and then I can let them live; there will be no need for the flood. I must give the people on earth this last chance. Therefore you must work away at the ark, which you will finish only when the time comes for the flood."

7

NOAH BUILDS THE ARK

That very night Noah fell into a deep sleep, and he dreamt that his great-grandfather Enoch came to him as the fiery angel Metatron. On a nearby table he saw Enoch put down a small chest made of sapphire that shone and gleamed with a brilliant light. "In that chest," said Enoch, "is a book of wisdom on a parchment scroll that the angel Raziel wrote long ago. That angel gave it to Adam, so that he might learn the ways of the Almighty. When Adam died, it disappeared from sight, for the Almighty wanted no common man to find so holy a book. But when I buried Adam in the double cave, there I found this book; and I took it with me to my secret home in the forest. It was from that I learned everything about nature, about heaven and earth. When I knew all the book could teach me, I hid it well; for I too had to make certain it would not fall into the hands of any unworthy person. Now it is time for *you* to read it, that you too may learn all the secrets of heaven and earth. Study it in holiness, and by its wisdom you will know how to build the ark and how to care for all the creatures that will come to live in it."

Enoch vanished; but when Noah awoke, there lay the radiant chest of sapphire on the table nearby. He began studying at once the parchment scroll he found inside, and he continued for days and weeks, until he knew every word written there. Then a new spirit of holiness settled upon him, and suddenly it was so very clear to him how to build the ark.

The Almighty had told him to make it of smoothed boards of gopher wood. Then he must begin with logs of that wood, which he could get only from trees. At once Noah went to a clear, unused stretch of land, and there he planted gopher trees by the many hundreds. Some people happened by, and seized by curiosity, they stopped to watch. "Why are you planting all those trees?" asked one of them.

In a clear voice Noah replied, "I will need the wood from their trunks when the trees are fully grown. For the Almighty, who created the world, has bidden me to build an ark, which can float on water. You see, He plans to bring a flood over the entire world, because the people in it are so wicked and bad. Then my family and I will be quite safe in the ark."

The handful of people only laughed. "Do you really believe," asked one of them, "that such a flood can come over the whole world? What utter nonsense. Are you sure you feel right in the head?" The rest of them laughed

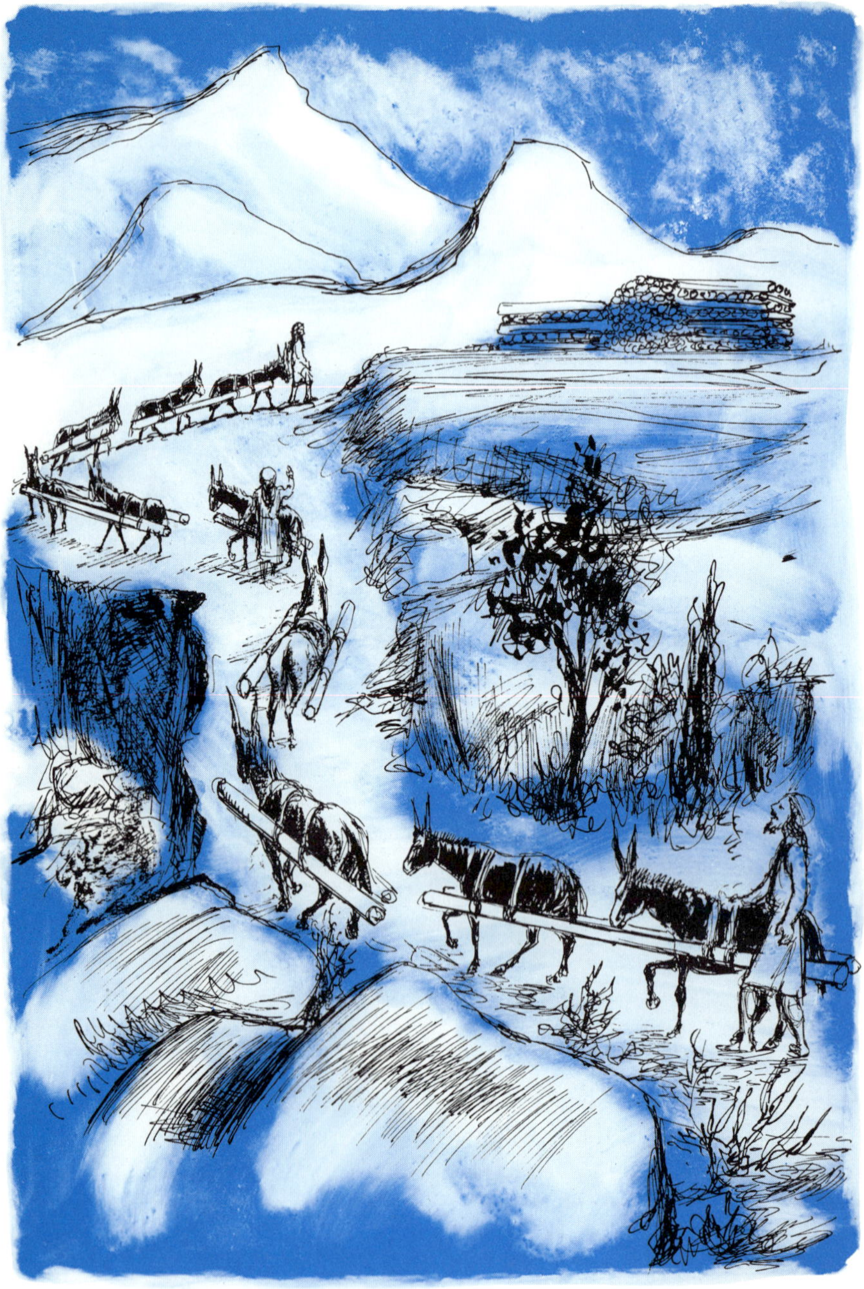

yet louder. Then another man spoke up: "I remember you. You went everywhere with that old man Methuselah, to warn us that some great disaster will come if we do not stop being so wicked. So now you say a tremendous *flood* will come; and you are building yourself an ark. Well, go ahead, if it makes you happy. We shall not stop you. After all, it is a harmless kind of foolishness." So laughing and chuckling, the people went on their way. And Noah continued with his work.

With his new, masterful knowledge from the *Book of Raziel,* he could make the trees grow rapidly, as he watered the ground day after day. Time and again people stopped to watch, drawn by curiosity; and when they in turn learned of his plan, they too answered with scorn. Paying no attention, Noah went on to cut the trees down when they were fully grown. From the tree trunks he made flat boards and planks; then he made their surfaces smooth and even.

Ready at least to build the ark, Noah loaded his planks and boards on many donkeys, to take them to the high plain where he was to set to work. He put the wood on a side, in a tremendous pile. And patiently, with absolute confidence, he began his task, marking off the measurements on the ground.

The Almighty had bidden him make the ark 300 cubits long, fifty cubits wide, and thirty cubits high. Now, the cubit is about eighteen inches, or a foot-and-a-half. So the ark should have been about 450 feet in length, seventy-five in width, and forty-five feet in height. But then it would have been far too small to hold all the animals and creatures that he was to take with him. From the *Book of Raziel,* however, Noah knew he was to use not the ordinary measure but a special "large cubit" that was much longer. Thus the ark would really be of tremendous size, easily able to hold all its animals and creatures. (Long afterward, in the land of Egypt that Noah's grandson Mizraim was to found, this special large measure would be known for thousands of years as the "Theban cubit," for it would be used in and about the Egyptian city of Thebes, to build the great, colossal pyramids that still stand today.)

For miles about in every direction, the high plain could be clearly seen. Noah had barely begun to build the framework when a great crowd gathered from all over, to watch in idle curiosity. For a long time they looked and whispered among themselves, trying to decide exactly what Noah meant to build. But never had they seen anyone do such work, and try as they would, they could not fathom his purpose.

At last one man stepped forward and spoke up: "Would you please tell me, you old benighted fool, just what you are doing? and why?"

Noah turned calmly from his work. "I am building an ark," he said.

"On, an ark," the man repeated, certain now that

Noah's mind was not working quite properly. "But what *is* an ark?" he asked with a mocking smile on his face.

"It is a kind of house," said Noah, "but it can stay afloat in water."

Others began to laugh aloud, certain that Noah was plainly a fool or a lunatic. And the man in front decided to ask more questions, expecting the conversation to become funnier as it went along. "Tell me," he asked in a tone of voice that he might have used to a little boy, "why will you need an ark? Do you expect to carry it to the ocean when you are finished, so that you can live on the water? Do you find it unpleasant to live on land because the earth is so firm and still under your feet and does not move about constantly like the ocean?" A smirk of pleasure covered his face as many laughed boisterously at his wit.

Noah waited for the laughter to die down. "I will not carry the ark to water," he replied. "I expect water to come here. When this ark is finished, the Almighty will bring a flood over the world—and then this ark will keep my family and me safe amid the rising water. But you too can be safe—all of you who stand here. Only give up the evil things you do; quit your lying and thieving and robbing; turn to the Almighty and obey Him— and no flood will come. Listen well, and tell this to your friends and neighbors. For as sure as I stand here before you, when this ark is ready the flood will come, and your dead carcasses will go floating on the water."

A jab of fear struck at the heart of the man in front, and he retorted in annoyance and anger, "Do you still believe there is an Almighty Ruler in heaven who will punish us with a disaster? You told us that before. Why do you not turn to *our* gods and worship our idols, as we do? They protect us no matter what we do." Grunts and murmurs of agreements rose from the people.

Still angry, the man in front continued, "Let me tell you something more, you benighted prophet of our doom: Do you think we fear a flood? Even if it were a flood of blazing fire instead of water, it would not matter a fig to us. We have an ointment, made from the blood of a certain species of salamander. When we cover our skin with it, no fire can harm us. And if this Almighty whom you worship should open the very windows of heaven and pour down tons of rainwater—do you think we would care? We have developed huge sponges which can absorb and hold tremendous amounts of water. You alone would need the ark then; we could all be quite safe without it. . . . Well, what else can this Almighty whom you worship do to bring a flood? Will he open the chasms in the earth to send water oozing and streaming up? We have huge, vast sheets of iron that can cover the ground completely, until hardly a drop can get through."

Among the listening and watching crowd stood many of the evil giants who had been born as sons to the fallen sinful angels. Now one of them strode forward, his head high above the rest. "Have you forgotten us —the 'tall boys' of the world?" he asked Noah with a sneer. "Let the world be flooded by all the water in heaven and beneath the ground: we giants would still have our heads above it. How could *we* ever be drowned? And if the ground should open a crack to let water well up from the deep, we giants would simply stand on the crack with our bare feet, and the opening would be covered."

A great cheer rose from the crowd at these words. Then the man in front spoke once more: "Build your ark as you wish, if it makes you happy. But spare us your speeches to warn us about a flood unless we change the way we live. We like the way we live, and we have no wish to change." The shouting continued a while; then the crowd slowly dispersed and scattered.

Noah shrugged and went back to work.

The years moved on, and Noah's three sons grew tall and strong. After a while, people watching the ark being built no longer saw Noah alone at work on the high plain. With him were his tall sons, helping faithfully. And when the time came for them to marry, they were wed to three granddaughters of Methuselah, born to his son Elyakim. For Elyakim was one of the few good men left on earth, and he had raised his three daughters in the ways of Enoch and Methuselah, far from the evil and violence that filled the world.

With his grown sons to help him, Noah found the work going faster. It would yet take years to finish, but not too many years. Steadily they worked, finishing the strong, thick walls and the roof. Then they put in the mighty cross-beams to make the walls and roof yet firmer: no matter how the flood might smash against the ark and batter it, it would never break and collapse.

Then Noah realized something else: the few good, kind people who remained on earth—members of his father's and grandfather's family—were beginning to die. The Almighty was true to His word: With the time for the flood approaching, old age came to these people, to take them peacefully to an eternal life of happiness. And as Noah reached the age of 595, Lamech his father died. Except for Noah and his family, the only good person left on earth was his grandfather Methuselah.

One other change happened in the last years before the flood, although Noah knew nothing of it. For a long time the fallen sinful angels had been yearning to be forgiven. They had once been proud and defiant, when they left heaven to live as men on earth. But now they saw what dreadful things their sons the giants did, and they were truly sorry for their sin. They wished they had never thought of leaving heaven.

As the time for the flood drew near, when the earth would be cleansed of the giants and all the evil they had brought, the Almighty took pity on the fallen sinful angels, and He allowed them to leave their lives on earth and become invisible angels once more. He could not let them return to heaven, however; for the rest of time they would have to exist between heaven and earth.

So the fallen angels too ended their lives on earth. One, however, was not forgiven. Their leader Azazel remained too proud and arrogant to ever be sorry for anything he had done. When all the others left earth to become true angels once more, Enoch came as the fiery angel Metatron, to bind Azazel in chains that no human eye could see, but which Azazel could never break. To a place far off in the wilderness he took Azazel, and there he cast him into a pit of sharp, jagged stones, where darkness would cover him forever.

With his great power, Azazel would survive the flood; but never again would he bring evil and violence to the world. Thousands of years later, when the people of Israel would live on their own land, they were to remember Azazel every year on *Yom Kippur* (the Day of Atonement), the holiest of all the days. For then, by the law of the Torah, they sacrificed a goat at a steep mountain in the wilderness, above the pit where Azazel is forever imprisoned. The Almighty wanted the Israelites to remember the fate that awaits even a powerful angel, if he remains sinful and defiant.

So the last years before the flood approached their end. On the high plain, Noah and his sons covered the ark, both inside and outside, with black melted pitch, to seal up every crack and crevice in the beams and

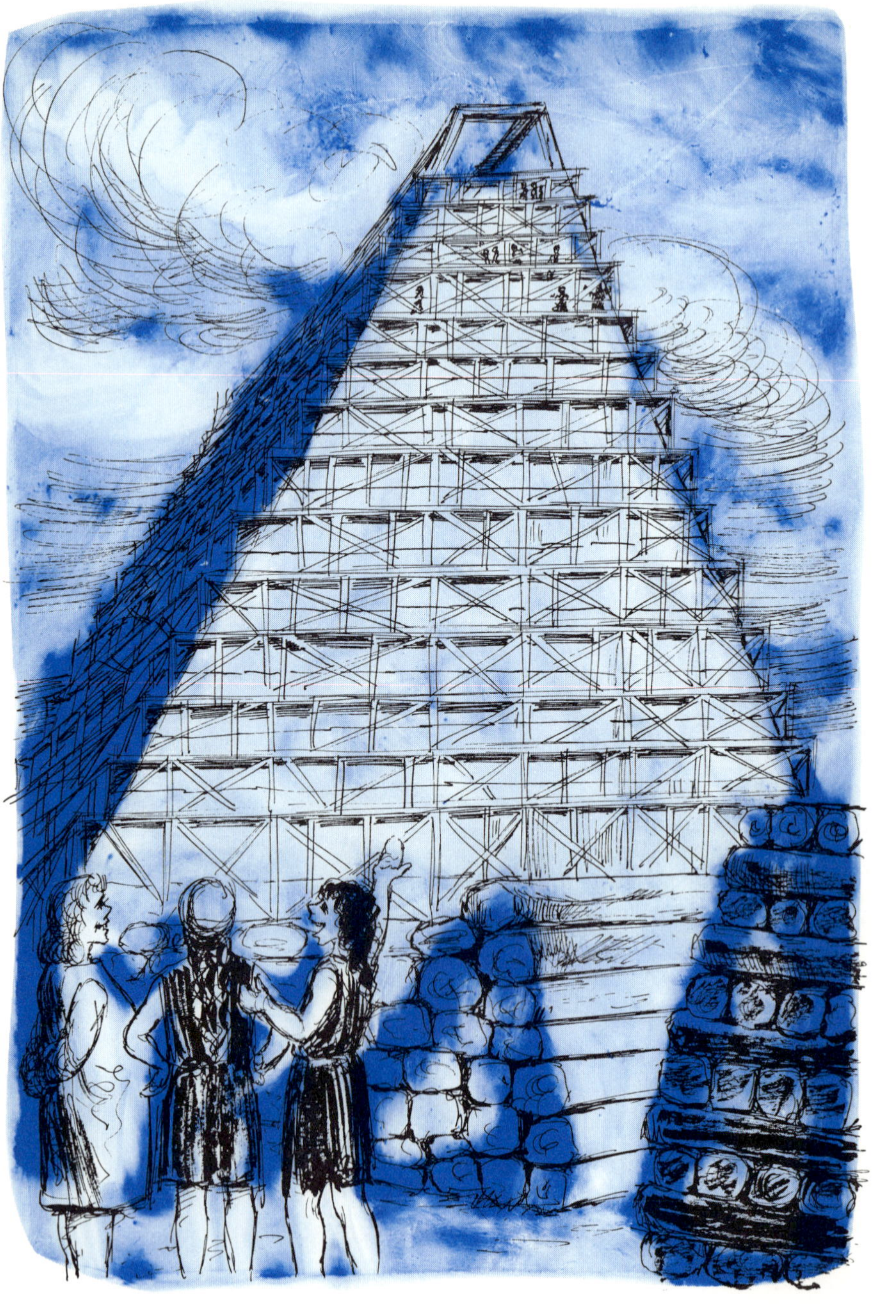

planks that formed the walls and the roof. When the heavy black pitch dried, no storm-wind or flood-water would ever get in.

Then Noah and his sons set to work *within* the ark, building sturdy floors to make decks or stories: one at the very bottom, one in the middle, and one beneath the sloping roof. Ladders were set beneath open hatchways, so that they could go easily from one deck to another. And last of all they divided the three decks into rooms and chambers, working from a plan Noah had made after the *Book of Raziel* had given him the wisdom to know all he had to build.

At last the work was done. Vastly more gigantic in shape than any house that man had ever built, the great ark lay on the high plain for all to see, gleaming pitch-black in the glorious light of the sun.

Together the family stood in its shadow—Noah with his dear wife, and the three sons with their wives—and they gazed at this sturdy "home" that would ride safely through the wildest storm and flood. A great happiness filled their hearts, to see it finished at long last. But they were also filled with awe at the sight of all that they—the father and the three sons—had done. For the ark was magnificent, far better than they had ever thought to make it. (Noah knew, though, that they had *not* built it alone. Whenever he found a plank too heavy to lift, he would suddenly feel it being lifted for him. Whenever a beam was too heavy to move, he would only have to touch it to see it gliding into place. With certain tools he had always been clumsy; yet when he used them in building the ark, they seemed to work for him with a skill of their own. Noah knew that all along, Heaven helped him in its own invisible way.)

Long did they keep gazing at the ark, as though they could not see enough of it. In the evening the family made a small feast, to which Noah brought his grandfather Methuselah—although he was now a very old man, who could walk only with Noah's help. For they wished to celebrate and to give thanks to the Almighty, after this day that they would always remember.

8

SEVEN LAST DAYS

The very next morning, Noah awoke with a sense of expectation; though exactly what would happen this day, he did not know. Not only was the ark ready after many years of building, but this day Noah became 600 years old. It was time, he knew, for the flood; perhaps it would soon begin. For in all the long years that he had worked on the ark, untold masses had come to watch; he had warned them all—and pleaded with them to become good. And all had scoffed and sneered. Not one had changed for the better.

Noah stepped out of his cottage and looked up at the sky. To his amazement, he heard a great commotion in heaven. As he listened he understood, by the wisdom that the *Book of Raziel* had given him, what the tumult and commotion meant: Angels in heaven were weeping and mourning because his grandfather Methuselah was no longer alive. His grandfather was perhaps the holiest man of his time, for he had studied many years with Enoch, his own father. He lived to the age of 969, longer than any other human being—and now the angels wept because his life on earth had ended.

Sadly Noah took his three grown sons and went to his grandfather's cottage, so that they could bury his body with honor. Now that Methuselah was gone, the flood was sure to come.

But as Noah and his sons reached his grandfather's cottage, an astonishing sight met their eyes: All about the cottage were gathered animals of every kind—and they too mourned and wailed for the holy man who had died. (These were animals which had not turned evil, that were to live with Noah in the ark through all the days of the flood.)

As his sons and he made their way through the mournful creatures, so that they could get on with the burial, people began gathering from everywhere, attracted by the sight and sound of the wailing animals. Slowly Noah and his sons left the cottage to begin the funeral, and the people realized what had happened. At last they understood what a good man Methuselah must have been, if even the animals wept for him. So the human beings decided to mourn for him too, and they followed Noah and his sons to pay a last honor to Methuselah.

It is told that the Almighty was pleased to see this. The flood should have begun that very day; but because those on earth wanted to honor Methuselah at his death, He kept the flood back a week, so that for seven days the people of the world could mourn and grieve for the holy man.

For those seven days, the ways of nature were entirely changed: The people on earth saw the sun rise in the west and set in the east. Never had the weather been so fair; and everywhere people found the most delicious fruit in their gardens, whose taste could have come only from Paradise. Thus the Almighty tried for the last time to get the humans on earth to give up their evil. He hoped they would realize in these seven days that everything was in His power, and life on earth could easily be a Paradise if they obeyed Him.

But the human beings on earth did not change. Wicked they were, and wicked they remained, their faces cruel and hard as hawks.

It was on the very first of those seven days, soon after he had brought the body of Methuselah to its final resting-place, that Noah heard the words of the Almighty once more: "Go into the ark, you and all your household; for I have seen that you alone are virtuous and good before Me, without guilt, in this generation. Take with you seven pairs—each pair a male and its mate—of every animal that is clean and pure. And of every kind that I consider unclean, impure, take only two—a male and its mate. Do the same with the birds of the sky: take seven pairs, each a male and its mate, of every kind that is pure and clean, and one pair of every other sort—

so that each kind of animal can go on bearing young, and thus will remain alive on the face of the earth" (Genesis 7:1-3).

Noah nodded in understanding, as the words of the Almighty continued: "For I am waiting yet another seven days, while the people on earth mourn the death of Methuselah. If they change for the better, they will be spared. If they do not, then seven days from now I will send rain down upon the earth—rain, for forty days and forty nights; and thus shall I blot out from the face of the earth the whole realm of living creatures that I have made" (Genesis 7:4).

"O mighty Ruler of the world," said Noah, "have I then the power to gather all the beasts and birds and creatures for the ark? There are hundreds upon hundreds of them, and I am no hunter. And even if I had the power, the flood is to begin in seven days; would I have time enough?"

The Almighty's answer came: "Remain at the ark, for all the creatures will come of themselves. Only make sure you let in no animal which men have taught to be as evil as themselves."

No sooner had Noah heard this than the pairs of living beings began indeed to arrive. With fluttering wings and loud cries, the birds flew in through the open door. But the four-legged animals stayed on the high plain waiting, as the door of the ark was far above the ground. With his three sons to help him, Noah set to work building a little wooden path, a ramp of timber strong enough to bear the largest elephant and rhinoceros. This he set to lead from the ground to the ark's door—and up the animals marched on it.

Never had Noah realized there were so many different kinds of living beings in the world; the varieties were simply endless, and utterly amazing. The beasts were of every size—enormously large, medium, and tiny—and many came with horns, tusks, or unusual fur. Every single species came with its mate: the tiger, zebra and horse; the dog, cat and mouse; and so many more.

So too the birds came in all sizes and colors, some with fantastic beaks, spectacular feathers, or unbelievably long necks. From the fierce giant eagle to the little wren, each flew in with its mate—among them the heron and falcon, lark and thrush, the strutting peacock and the hook-beaked pelican. As for the insects, they were often too strange and peculiar to ever be described.

Thus the creatures of the world came to the ark, walking, hopping, flying or crawling. Of reptiles alone, there were 365 different types. All in all, well over a thousand species of creatures came of their own free will, as Noah watched in endless astonishment.

For a while he wondered where he should put them and how he should arrange them. But when he looked inside, he saw he need not bother himself. As the Almighty had bidden him, he had made three decks or floors in the ark. No creature now went to the highest

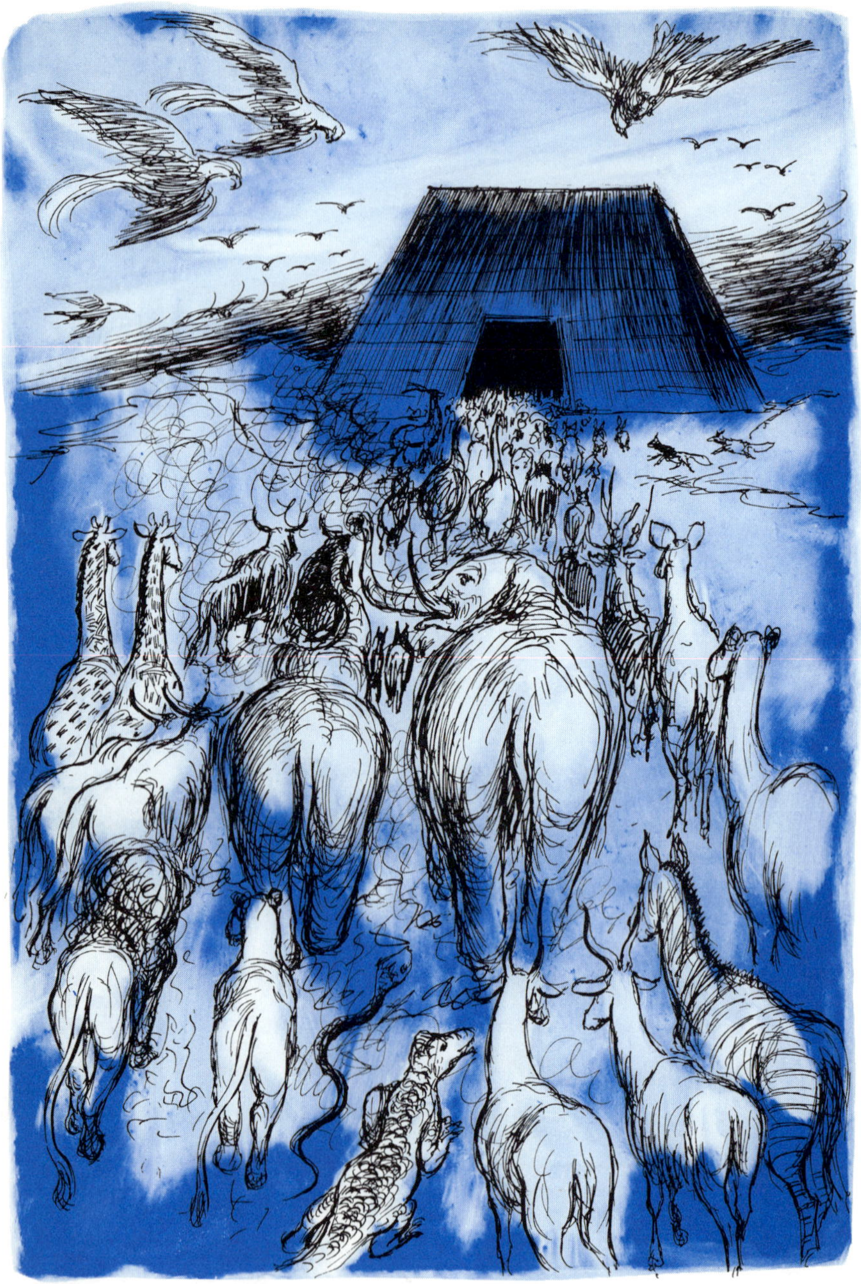

deck, as all went to the middle one. So the lowest deck was left free for the garbage, waste and refuse that would collect in the many days of the flood; and the upper deck remained for the human beings—Noah, his sons, and their wives—and for the food supply.

As Noah looked through the middle deck, he saw that there too a Divine wisdom guided the creatures. Every pair found a place to stay comfortably: the beasts sat or walked about on the floor, while the birds perched on the great cross-beams. And if two kinds of animals were natural enemies, they generally managed to find places far away from each other, so that both could stay peacefully. If it happened that natural enemies had to remain near one another, they forgot their instincts and habits, and rested quietly.

Yet not always did things go smoothly. Often too many animals of one kind came, and he could not admit them all. Then, by the wisdom of the *Book of Raziel,* he used a simple test: Those which lay down before him, he let into the ark—for so he knew that they were docile and peaceful, and had not turned evil. Those which remained standing before him, he drove away—for they had learned from wicked men to be haughty and proud.

However, when a lioness came with her two lion cubs, Noah was puzzled: for all three crouched down, yet he could let only two enter. Then the two young ones began to struggle with the mother, until she arose and stood next to them. At that Noah drove the lioness away and let the cubs go in.

Many pairs of beasts that came were young and small, rather than fully grown, so that they fit more readily into the ark. But then a male and female *r'em* came—a species of wild ox or bison—and Noah was perplexed, not knowing at all what to do. The pair were very young too; yet so huge were they, and so tremendous their horns, that they could not fit on the middle deck of the ark. For days they remained outside, waiting. On the morning of the seventh day, Noah took them to the side of the ark and tied their horns to it tightly. In the wall of the ark he made two holes, so that they could just fit their faces through, to breath and take food. So they would have to stay during the entire flood, towed along in the water by the ark.

The last difficulty in those seven days came to Noah when a giant named Og approached him. With tears in his eyes Og pleaded for a place in the ark—for of all the giants born to the sinful angels he alone had never liked being evil. Now he realized that Noah was telling the truth about the approaching flood. "Save me," he begged Noah. "Let me stay somewhere, anywhere in the ark—and I swear that I and any children I will have shall be slaves to you and your children, for all time. As your slaves, we will be unable to do any more evil."

Noah could not turn him away. Yet how could so tall a giant fit inside the ark? There was only one thing to be done: Og would have to sit *atop* the ark, one foot on each of the roof's two sides that came sloping up to end a cubit away from each other. He would be thoroughly wet as long as the flood lasted, but at least the ark would keep him from drowning in the water that would rise above the ground. Near the roof's narrow top Noah made a large hole that could be opened and shut tight again. Once a day Noah would open it to hand Og his food. The rest of the time it would remain shut.

When the seven days ended, the creatures that belonged in the ark sat snugly in their places. The next morning began in bright warm sunlight. Then suddenly, without warning, the sun was darkened, and the very foundations of the earth seemed to tremble, as lightning tore the sky in jagged flashes and thunder boomed in savage outbursts. Never before had a storm like this struck the world. And even then the Almighty waited, to see if the people on earth would learn anything from these awesome sights and sounds, and perhaps they would give up their wicked ways at last. But their fierce cruel hearts would never soften.

The amazing storm ended as suddenly as it had come. A light rain began to fall softly—nothing more. For even then, at the last possible moment, if only the people of the world were to pray to the Almighty, the gentle rain alone would continue, as a blessing, to water the farmlands of the earth. No flood would come. Yet in all the world no one gave a thought to the darkened sun or the rain—no one, except Noah.

"Shem! Ham! Japheth!" he called; and his three sons came to him. "Is everything ready in the ark?" he asked. "Have you put in all the supplies of food?"

"Yes, father," replied Shem. "All has been ready for days."

"Very well," said Noah. "Let each of you bring his wife, and we will enter. This is no ordinary winter rain, but the beginning of the flood." Even as he spoke, a chill wind spread across the plains and fields, raising dust and sand into the air. He went swiftly for Naamah his wife, and they walked to the ark. But at the wooden path that led from the ground to the door, they had to wait, together with his three sons and their wives. For until this final moment the creatures of the world kept arriving in pairs, and now the last of them went running, crawling or slithering up the wooden ramp. And as Noah and his family waited patiently, the rain-water began to gather and remain on the ground. It reached to their ankles before they were finally able to go in.

Once inside, they hurled away the wooden ramp that led from ground to ark; and not a moment too soon did they close the door behind them. For at that very instant, people came running up by the thousands. Wild blinding lightning flashed again in great zigzags through the heavens, and thunder began to roar and echo once more. Stronger than ever was the howling wind, as the gentle rain became a mighty downpour. Now the people knew it was no ordinary rainstorm, but the start of the flood that Noah had kept foretelling and promising. So they came dashing wildly up the high plain to the ark.

Their first move was to lift the wooden ramp and set it back in place, making it lead again from the ground to the ark's door. Then up the ramp they ran. Frightened for their lives, they desperately pulled and pushed at the door, determined to save themselves at all costs by getting inside. Yet all their straining and tugging was for nothing. Once Noah closed the door, the Almighty sealed it shut, and no power on earth could open it.

"Noah!" cried the people's spokesman. "Open the door and let us into the ark with you. Do not let us die!"

"Did you not rebel against the Almighty, all of you?" shouted Noah through the door. "You always joked and sneered when I warned you about Him. Your hard insolent faces laughed at me, for as you told me in your scorn, you did not believe He even exists. Then He *must* bring this punishment upon you, which will destroy you and remove you from the face of the earth —so that you will finally learn that He *does* exist. And pray tell me: why did you wait till now to plead for your lives? Did Methuselah and I not warn you for 120 years that exactly this disaster would come? For so long you would not listen to the Almighty's words—and now you want to be left alive on earth!"

"But we are here now," begged the spokesman, "ready to heed the Almighty and obey Him. Just open the door for us, that we may live and not die."

"Only now do you wish to cling to Him," retorted Noah, "because you see what terrible disaster faces you. In all the 120 years you kept boasting that no harm from earth or heaven could ever befall you. Why did you not seek to know Him in all the time. He waited for you? If you come only now to speak this way, it is because you care nothing about the great evil you have done; you have no true wish to change; seeing death ahead, you merely wish to save yourselves. So the Almighty will not listen to you: no attention will He pay to your voices this day. Go back, I tell you, for you will accomplish nothing here!"

With that, Noah and his family went to their rooms on the upper deck. And outside, the water on the ground kept rising. Furious with anger over their plight, the thousands decided to break down the door and enter by force. Someone found a beam of timber, and those in front eagerly seized it. Shouting defiance, they prepared to use it as a battering ram and smash its narrowed end against the door.

Behind the ark, however, stood a great horde of lions, tigers, leopards, and other wild beasts. During the last seven days they had gathered, sensing by some deep instinct that a terrible disaster was coming, when they could be safe only in the ark. Though Noah turned them away (for he could let in only two of each kind), they stayed behind the ark, not knowing where else to go.

Now they moved. As though by Divine command, they lunged forward with mighty roars and bellows, and leaped onto the wooden ramp to attack the men of evil. Instantly they dropped their beam of timber; gone was every thought of breaking into the ark, as they jumped and ran to escape the ferocious jungle animals. When the wild beasts were done, many lay dead and mangled; the rest had scattered in every direction.

With their powerful heads and shoulders, the wild beasts pushed the wooden ramp far from the ark, until it lay on the ground (as before), a good distance away. Then there was only the sound of the heavy, steady downpour.

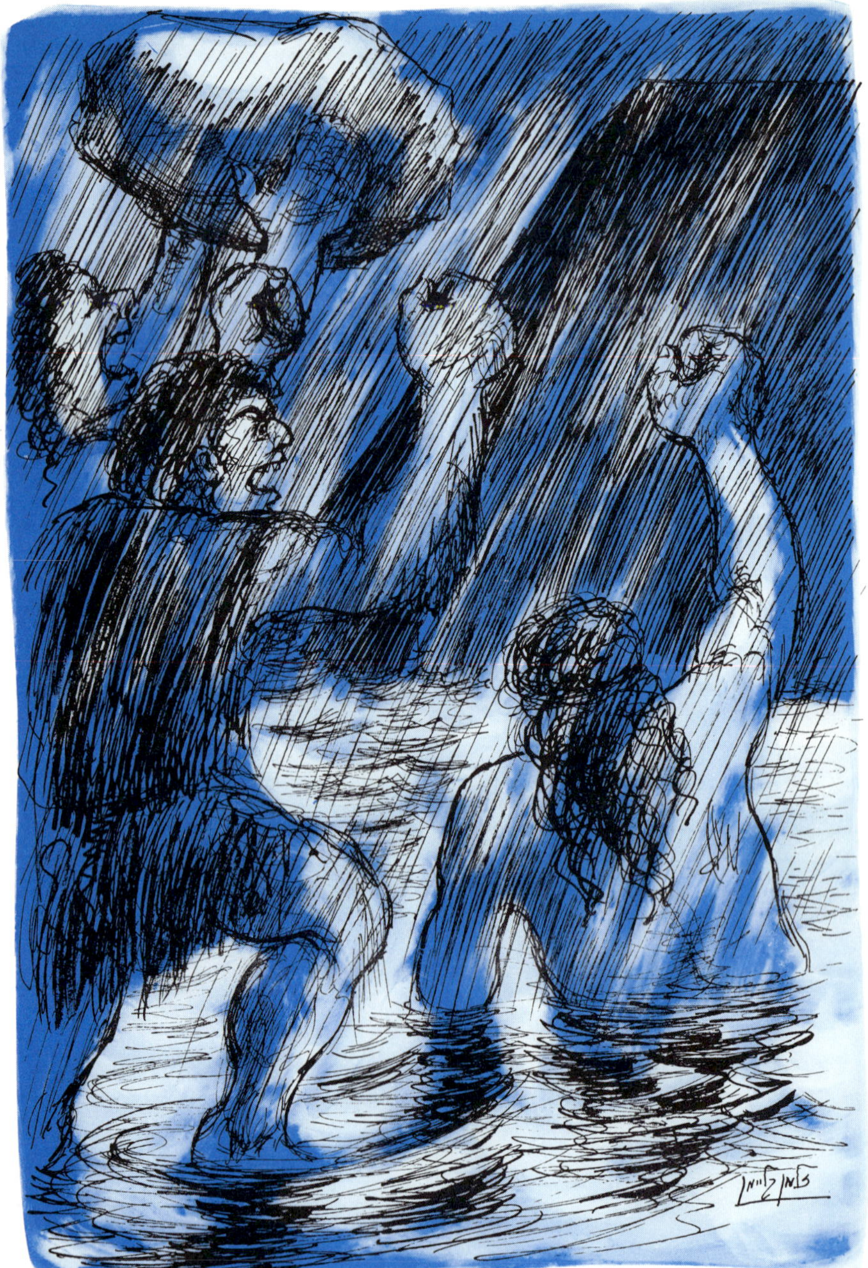

9

THE FLOOD

On the seventeenth day of Ḥeshvan, the second month (as the Hebrew year is reckoned), the torrent of rain began. It was to continue through forty days and night of darkness—for in all that time, no sun, moon or stars ever appeared. It is told that from a group of stars called the constellation Pleiades, the Almighty removed two; and where these two stars were missing, it was then as though two windows had been opened up in heaven, through which the enormous downpour could rain steadily for the forty days and nights, without a stop. (It is further told that when the time came for the furious rain to end, the Almighty could not put back the same two stars, for the spaces had become too large to hold them. So He put in two larger stars from the Bear constellation. For this reason—it is said—whenever astronomers watch the sky, the second constellation of stars always looks like a bear chasing the Pleiades group: The "mother bear" is trying to get her two "children" back.)

But the flood-water came not only from above. Far down in the earth, great holes and cracks opened, and fountains of water came surging, gushing, welling up from the depths. Higher and higher rose the streams that gathered and covered the ground, until no one could be mistaken any longer: It was a terrible flood, spread across the whole world. . . . And people began to drown.

To the very end, the people of the world remained as wicked as ever. As soon as some began to drown, others seized their bodies and used them to stuff up the holes deep in the ground from which the mighty fountains of water were welling and gushing up. And when they could not find enough bodies, stronger people killed off the weaker, so that they could block up the holes with them.

Yet all was to no avail. For a brief moment an opening in the ground might be blocked up; but the fountains of water pushed up from the deep with such force that they thrust out anything in their path, or they found another way to pour out of the earth.

The Almighty, however, notices everything. When He saw that even in the face of death the earth's people cruelly killed neighbors and friends to try to save themselves, He sent a flood of fire for a moment amid the flood of water. The water became scalding hot—and the vicious murderers died instantly.

For a good while the giants of the earth felt no fear. As they had boasted to Noah, they were certain that no flood of rain-water could drown them, for they were too tall; and if streams came welling up from the ground, they were ready to block up the cracks and openings with their enormous feet. This they tried to do now—and it was no use. Stand as they would, the mighty fountains of water found some way of coming up from the depths of the earth.

Others had boasted, too, of gigantic sponges that could absorb flood-water, and of great sheets of iron that could cover the ground and keep water from flowing out. Now the sponges were of no help—for however much they absorbed and held, more rain kept falling. And so strong was the thrust of the well-springs from below that they heaved aside the huge sheets of iron.

At last the giants were frightened too. With their mighty strides, many headed for the ark, ready to seize it and use it to save themselves. Sure of their strength, they were certain that nothing could stop them.

It was at the moment their huge hands touched the ark that the Almighty sent the flash of fire amidst the water for an instant. They had boasted to Noah of a special ointment which kept the skin safe from fire. There was never a chance for them to get the ointment and use it. The sudden fire brought scalding heat to the water that now lay on the ground as high as their waist. One after another came lunging toward the door of the ark to wrench it open—and one after another, they crumpled and fell in the unbearable heat of the flood-water. And they perished, as the ark stood calm and still on the high plain.

In the grim, darkened world that showed no sun, moon or stars, the flood-waters rose steadily on the ground, until life on earth ended. As man and animal had lived without pity or kindness, so did the stormy raging water bring death to all, without pity or mercy. Gone were the sons and descendants of Cain, who had spread evil in the world ever since he murdered his brother Abel. For so ferocious were the raging flood-waters that even mill-stones (used for grinding grain into flour) were shattered to bits.

Only in the ark did humans and creatures yet live. And here and there some giants still roamed, as they kept their heads above the water. But the heavy downpour kept on, and well-springs gushed without stop from the depths of the earth; and the level of the flood-water rose higher and higher. The last remaining giants strode to the highest mountain they could find, and climbed to its very top. There they stood towering high above the ground; turning toward heaven, they shouted defiance to the Almighty. For how could the flood drown them if their heads were so high up?

They were mistaken. As the waters came without a stop, from above and below, for forty days and forty nights, they reached at last a level of fifteen cubits (about

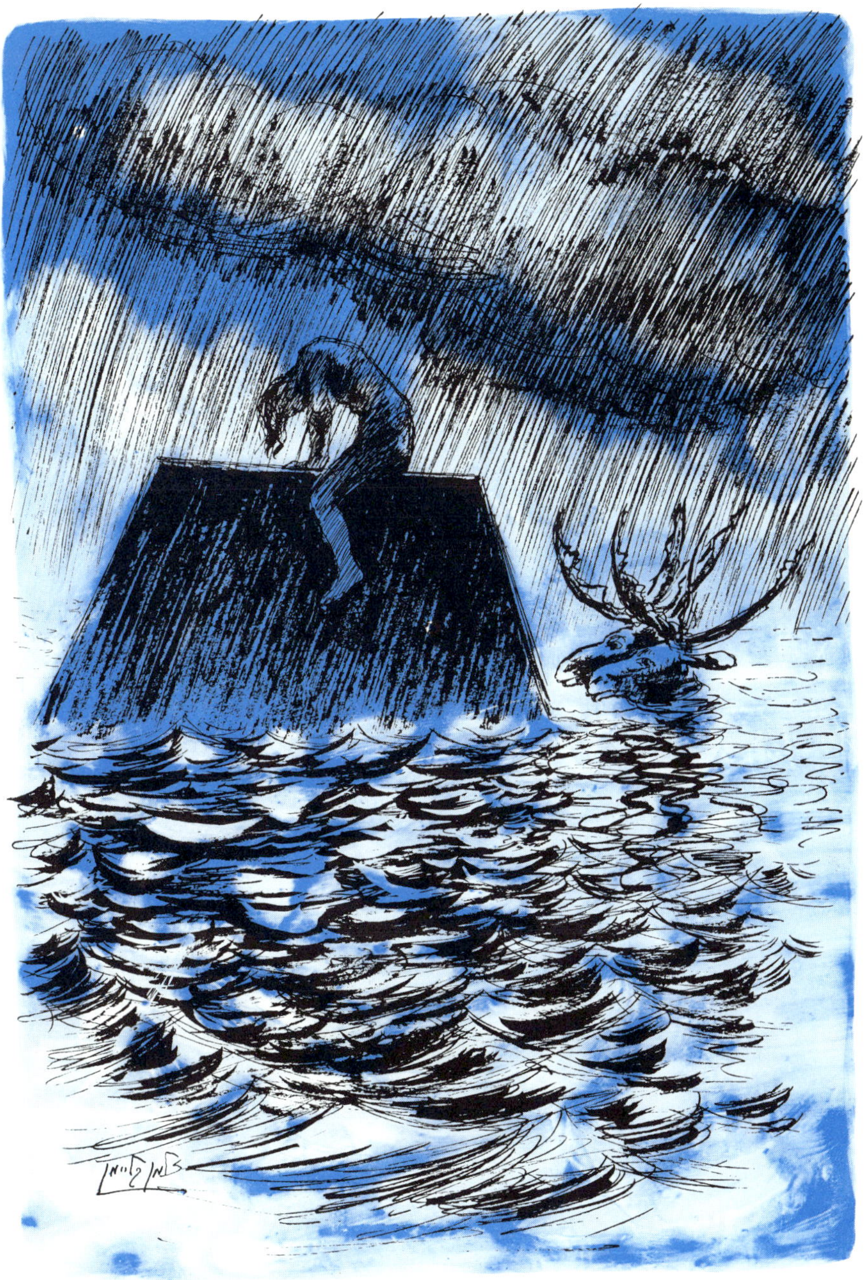

twenty-two and a half feet) above the tall mountain on which they stood. And even these giants died.

Of all the giants, Og alone remained—the only one who felt truly sorry for his bad deeds. He sat securely on the roof of the ark as it moved and swayed in the water. Everywhere he looked, he saw nothing but the fierce swirling flood. Nowhere could he see any living creatures or houses, or even trees. There was nothing but water all over the earth. And when he grew tired of looking at it, he would watch the pair of wild oxen or bisons called *r'em* that were tied by their tremendous antlers to the ark, so they could swim along behind. The foaming, churning waves that their feet kicked up were miles in length, rising as high as hills.

In all this time, the people and creatures inside the ark were as if in a strange little world of their own—a little world far different from the one they had known before, and different from the flooded lifeless realm that now existed outside the ark.

Even if Noah opened the blocked-up window for a moment, no light came in from a world that no longer say any sun, moon or stars. Yet the creatures in the ark did not have to live in the dark. High up, directly under the roof, he placed the parchment scroll of the *Book of Raziel* (the book that had given him so much knowledge and wisdom) in its sapphire chest. By day the sapphire shone and sparkled with such radiant light that it seemed as if a little sun were blazing there. And when night came, the glorious light of the sapphire softened and dimmed, so that no sleeping creature was kept awake.

Noah and his sons, however, were to get precious little sleep in their many months in the ark. For there were day creatures (which slept at night) and night creatures (which slept by day), and each had to be given its food at its proper time. Nor could all the day creatures be fed at once and all the night creatures at once. Some grew hungry in the second hour, some in the third, and so on. The *Book of Raziel* had given Noah wisdom enough to know exactly when to bring each creature its meal. He himself took charge of the wild beasts; Shem dealt with tame domestic animals, such as dogs and cows, which always lived with people; Ham had the duty to feed the many different kinds of birds; while Japheth took care of the reptiles, such as snakes, lizards and alligators.

While they were in the ark, Noah and his sons were much too busy to think about it. Only afterward did they realize what miracles the Almighty brought for them. In all their days and nights in the ark, they could nap sometimes for five minutes, sometimes for half an hour—never more than an hour. There were too many creatures to feed. Yet their health did not suffer, for the Almighty gave them strength, and they remained fine and well.

By another miracle, the creatures in the ark stayed calm and tame, though many of them were wild and dangerous in ordinary life, ready to attack and destroy any strange animal or human being that came near. Thus Noah and his three sons were able to move freely about on the middle deck, where all the creatures stayed, to bring them their food. Many would growl and look up with suspicious eyes; but none attacked. Even if one of the four men stepped on an animal's tail or paw by accident, it would only yelp or howl, but nothing more.

Once, though, an animal broke this rule. One morning Noah forgot completely about the lions, and as he fed the other wild beasts, the two lion cubs grew very hungry. At last a roar from the male lion reminded him, and he went running to bring the pair their food. So angry was the male cub (for after all, the lion is the king of the animals) that it attacked Noah in the hip; and for a long time afterward he walked with a limp.

And it is told that at another time one other creature forgot to be calm and quiet. Once (it is said) one young cat found itself sitting near a mouse. Its proper place to sit was far off in another corner; but cats are incurably curious about any new place where they happen to be; and they are known to be rather foolish and stupid animals, which cannot remember well what they ought to do. So it was that this particular cat went roaming, and came to rest, with its tail idly swishing, quite near the mouse.

Its eyes were narrow slits, and it appeared to be

more dreaming than awake. Yet the young cat kept watching the mouse carefully, and its mind was working away. "It seems to me," thought the larger animal, "that my ancestors have always used such creatures for food. Then it should be quite proper for me to catch it and have a little snack."

So thinking and musing, the cat pounced suddenly and swiftly. But fast as this creature was, the mouse was faster, and in the twinkling of an eye it scampered away, missing the cat's paws by a bare quarter of an inch. The cat, however, went after it, and the two were off on a merry chase. Fore and aft, back and forth they raced across the middle deck, among all the other creatures. The mouse knew what it needed: a hole in a wall somewhere, large enough to let it through, but too small for the cat. But where could it find a hole in an ark of solid wood, built to keep out the raging flood-waters?

Then a little miracle happened. As the mouse scampered along, it chanced to see a knot in a beam of wood. Quickly it pulled out the knot with its sharp teeth; and to its great relief, there was a little hole behind the knot, in the beam of timber. In a flash the mouse wriggled through, and not a moment too soon. For there was the cat, sniffing carefully at the tiny opening.

Desperately the mouse tried to crawl further inside the beam, but there was barely enough room to crouch in the hole. And as the cat realized that its prey was right there, it put a paw into the opening, with the claws uncovered, as far as it could. The mouse opened its mouth at once, hoping the paw would simply enter its mouth and find nothing to touch, and the cat would then withdraw its foot and go away. But the little creature's mouth was too small, and the cat's claws made a tear in the cheeks, on either side. In its deep pain, the mouse waited, perfectly still—until the cat realized it could do no more; and tired of waiting at the hole, it went back to its place.

When the little mouse sensed that night had fallen, it felt safe enough to come out; and it ran at once to Noah with tiny squeaks. Having studied the *Book of Raziel* thoroughly, Noah forgot nothing of all its immense wisdom and knowledge. One of its chapters had taught him the language of every beast and bird in the world. So he understood now the tiny squeaks of the little creature before him: The mouse was asking him to sew up the tear in its cheeks, that it might be healed.

"Go," said Noah, "and bring me a fine strong thread from the tail of a horse, and I will do as you wish."

On its tiny feet the mouse went back to the middle deck, where it made its way to the pair of horses. Both these fine, handsome animals were sound asleep. With its sharp teeth the mouse cut off a strong silken hair from the tail of one; the thread in its mouth, the little creature returned to Noah.

The pain was sharp and intense, yet the mouse

lay still as Noah worked with deft, skilled fingers. At last the torn cheeks were sewn with fine stitches, and the mouse went off to find comfort and final healing in sleep. (So it happens, people say, that to this day there is a little line like a seam on either side of a mouse's mouth.)

That night Noah fastened a leash about the neck of the cat, which he tied fast to a beam, to make sure the creature went roaming no more about the deck.

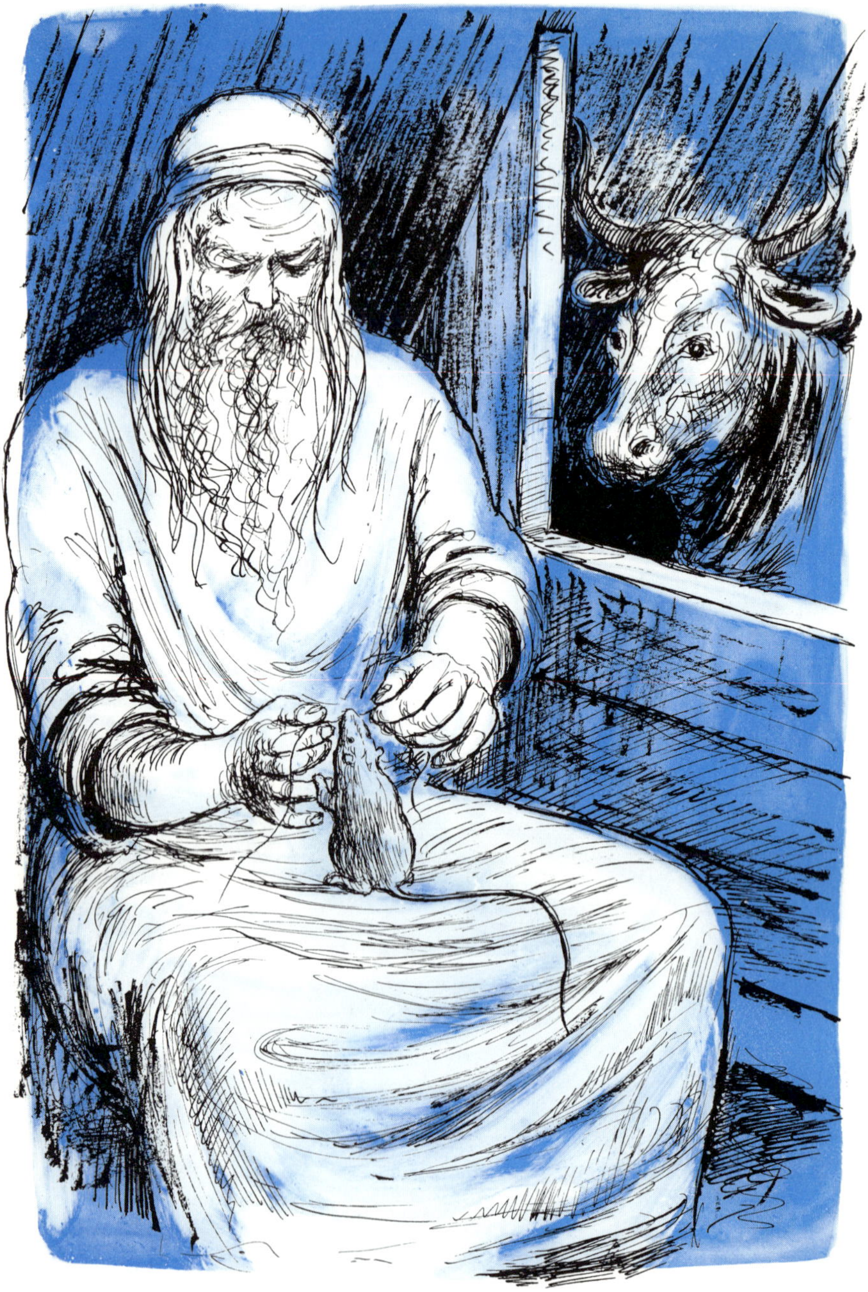

10

AS THE ARK FLOATED ON

If Noah and his sons never had enough sleep in the ark, having to feed all the different creatures through the day and the night, at least they had enough food for all. For the *Book of Raziel* had given him the great wisdom to know what to prepare for every bird and beast, insect and reptile. He had vine-twigs for the elephants, bean-plant leaves for the ravens, lupine seeds for the goats, hay for the cows, straw for the camels, oats for the horses, barley for the donkeys. On the upper deck, beneath the sloping roof, lay the great piles of food, enough to last a year and more. Especially plentiful were the heaps of grain and seed, fodder and hay —as well as a huge quantity of thick juicy figs. For many, many creatures could live on these foods.

Yet to every rule there is an exception. In the first days of the flood, Noah and his sons were happy, for they managed to give every creature its proper food in good time, and they saw the endless variety of creatures settle down in contentment. Then Noah happened to notice a pair of chameleons lying quietly in a corner. Had he not been looking closely there for something else, he would never have seen them—for the chameleon is a lizard that can take on the color of whatever it is lying on. The floor of the middle deck was made of wood planks—and the pair of chameleons had exactly the same color now.

"Japheth," called Noah, and his first son came to his side. "Have you noticed these creatures before?" Japheth had to look twice before he realized there were two lizards of some sort on the floor. "How could I see them?" he asked. "They are the very same color as the wood. How lucky that you noticed them now, father."

"Then no one has fed them," said Noah; "and we have already been in the ark three days. They must be starving."

"What sort of food shall I give them?" asked Japheth. Noah searched his mind carefully. Could he remember anything from the *Book of Raziel* that would give him the answer? Try as he would, he could remember nothing.

"We shall have to pray to the Almighty," he replied with a shrug, "to tell us. Now let us go on feeding the others." With that he cut a pomegranate in half, to give it to an animal nearby—and he caught his breath in surprise. For out of the pomegranate a maggot fell—a tiny grubby worm—and quick as a flash one of the chameleons scooped it up with a sharp little tongue.

"Well," said Noah, "now I know what these creatures will eat." Instantly he climbed the stairs to the upper deck. That morning he had kneaded a great mound of bran, that he used as food for some of the animals. In a dark corner of the upper dark lay a large piece of the bran that had been left over. Noah carried it over to the light—and smiled. For just as he had hoped, a whole group of maggots were breeding and festering in the moldy, rotting bran. Noah took it at once to the chameleons, and he watched the two speedily devour the maggots, to the last one.

As long as Noah remained in the ark, he always kneaded bran and let it stand, until maggots bred in it. So the two special lizards always had food.

Later that day his son Ham called him: "Father, one pair of birds is fast asleep. Shall I wake them?" Noah went to see. In a far corner of the middle deck two birds sat perched. They were a species called the phoenix, and both the male and female were indeed asleep. From the *Book of Raziel,* though, Noah knew the language of winged creatures; and he spoke and called to them until the male phoenix opened one eye. "Why are you both asleep?" asked Noah. "Is it not the time for you to eat?"

Replied the phoenix, "My mate and I saw how busy all of you are, because you have so many creatures to feed. Well, we have the power to sleep for a long time if we wish to, and then we do not need any food. So we have decided to remain asleep as long as we are here, in the ark. Then we will not add to your heavy burdens and cares."

Noah was touched by this thoughtfulness. "May it be the Almighty's will," he exclaimed, "that you shall live forever." And it is told that his blessing came true: All other creatures live on earth only till death comes; but the bird called the phoenix never dies.

So life went peacefully on for many days inside the ark, and neither the humans nor the creatures in all their great variety knew anything much about the flood raging outside. They could hear the heavy rain beating steadily on the roof amid the violent crashes of thunder; and faintly there came to their ears the furious rush of the mighty torrents that poured up from the depths of the earth. But life in the ark remained serene and quiet, broken only by the cries and barks of animals every now and then, or the trills and calls of the birds (beginning with the rooster's cry at the hour of dawn), or the occasional flutter of wings as birds changed their perches.

It was especially quiet as evening changed to full darkness, when the creatures of day already slept and the creatures of night were not yet awake. In that stillness, the nightingale alone sang on, recalling the beauty, splendor and warmth of the world before the flood—

the world that would thrive again when the torrent was over and gone.

This was life in the ark in the first days of the flood, when it yet stood firm on the high plain where Noah built it. But as the water rose steadily above the ground, it lifted this huge pitch-black wooden structure and sent it floating about, whichever way the flood moved it.

Were it able to float slowly and smoothly, all would have remained well in the ark. But the storm-winds were ferocious, and the fountains and well-springs from the depth of the earth sent their waters pouring, streaming with stupendous force. Everywhere the flood-water scurried, swirled and eddied about in a frenzy—and the ark was violently pushed and hurled in every possible direction. The poor creatures within were tossed and shaken like peas in a pot, until they hardly knew what to do with themselves. The lions roared, cows mooed, and wolves and dogs howled in misery. And the birds twittered and shrieked in alarm.

It was a dreadful bedlam of sound, as every animal told, in the voice nature had given it, of its agony and fear.

No less miserable were the people in the ark. Neither Noah nor his sons nor their wives could bear to be hurled and shaken constantly, and they wept in despair. "O mighty Ruler of the world," Noah prayed, "I beg You to rescue us, for we have not the strength to bear this sore trouble that has come upon us. On every side we are surrounded by billowing waves of death. Flood-waters from the dreaded depths attack us. Is then death coming to trap us too? for it already stares us in the face! Answer us, O Lord; answer us, and take us out of this misery. Listen to our prayer, be kind to us, and save us!"

The Almighty heeded his prayer. Although the rain and the well-springs poured their water for a full forty days and nights, from then on the ark found itself in calm places, moved gently by a steady wind that kept it away from the giant waves and roaring whirlpools.

After forty days and nights the rain stopped, as though heaven's windows were closed once more; and the great holes and cracks in the earth closed completely. The mighty fountains and well-springs no longer streamed up from them.

Now a terrible stillness settled over the world. Silent were the darkened heavens, as no storm-clouds or lightning burst any longer; and quiet lay the earth under the massive blanket of water that covered it utterly. And of all the life that had teemed and swarmed so busily in the world, not a creature was left. The earth was free of the evil that its human beings had brought.

On the twenty-seventh of Kislev (the third month of the Jewish year), forty days and nights after the flood had begun, the waters stopped pouring from above and below. But for the next 150 days (until the first of Sivan, the Jewish year's ninth month) the blanket of water remained exactly the same: If it did not rise any higher, neither did it go any lower. Inside the ark, Noah and his sons and their wives went on living patiently, day after day. They knew it would be a long while before they could hope to see dry land again. There was simply too much water.

The 150 days came to an end. Then (from the first of Sivan) the great "ocean" that covered the earth began to slowly disappear. Water at the top evaporated into the air. Water at the bottom began to find its way back into the depths of the earth. Each day the great ocean that covered the world became lower by a few inches. And as the water level became lower, so did the ark come ever so closer to earth—until, on the seventeenth of Sivan, it came to a standstill. For the bottom of the ark landed on the tall mountains of Ararat, in the land of Armenia.

Originally, the flood-waters had risen to a height of fifteen cubits above the mountains. Now they had gone down by four cubits, so that eleven cubits of water still surrounded the ark. But to the people and creatures inside the ark that did not matter. They simply felt a great relief at the change. Now they no longer felt the floor forever shaking, moving, rocking under them—never still, because the water constantly tossed it ever so slightly about. And no longer did they feel the ark moving off somewhere—in what direction, heaven alone knew. Now they felt as though on dry land.

From inside the ark Noah had no way of knowing where they were, or how much water remained in the world outside. But he shrewdly guessed that many months would have to pass before he could hope to step out of this floating home and find dry land outside. Yet he dearly wished he would not have to wait too much. His sons were young, strong and healthy, and they could easily bear their hard life in the ark. But he was an older man; and having to work night and day to feed the animals, with very little time for sleep, he found he was too weary to bear the cold. From the great ocean of flood water, a moist chill always seeped into the ark; no matter how warm the clothing he wore, Noah found he was always shivering with cold. It was painful for him to move about, and he often groaned as he walked to bring the animals their food. How he hoped for the day he could leave this floating "home on water," and let the shining sun bring him warmth.

A little while later, Noah went at last to open the window, the opening in the ark that had always been kept shut. It was only forty days since the flood-water over the world had begun to flow back into the earth and slowly disappear. And only twenty-four days ago the ark had landed on the mountains of Ararat, to remain perfectly still. But Noah was impatient to see what the world outside looked like.

Eagerly he put his head through the opening, and looked carefully about. No longer was the world so dark and gloomy as in the forty days when the flood-waters poured in torrents. But the sky remained a dull leaden grey, as a massive layer of cloud completely hid the sun.

Noah looked far and wide, longing to see a bit of dry land. Alas, all he could see was water, water everywhere—dark and grim under the sunless sky that looked like lead. Winds blew across, and chilled him to the bone, until he ached more than ever from the cold. How long would it yet be, he wondered with a groan of pain, before solid ground appeared?

Then he looked straight down, and a gleam of hope shone in his eyes: For he realized that the level of the flood-water was no longer high at all. It covered perhaps a sixth of the ark's height, no more. The rest of the ark rose clear above it. Could it be, thought Noah, that in other parts of the world dry land was beginning to appear?

Noah had an idea: he would send out the raven, the largest and boldest of the crows. Of all the birds, it was one of the most intelligent; and only the raven and the dove had the power to sense something of the future. Let the raven now fly about in the world; then it could return and tell him all it had seen. For thanks to the *Book of Raziel,* Noah knew the language of birds.

11

THE WINGED MESSENGERS

Still moaning with pain from the cold moist air, Noah made his way slowly to the middle deck. A sixth sense must have warned the raven, for as the master of the ark approached, it flew from its perch to hide behind the great bald eagle. But Noah noticed it, and he ordered it down at once. Its beady eyes glaring with anger, the jet-black bird fluttered its wings and settled on his arm.

"Your Master the Almighty hates me," said the raven; "and neither do you have any liking for me."

"Why do you say that?" asked Noah.

"Your Master ordered you to take in seven pairs of every animal that He considers clean and pure, but only one pair of every other kind. There are but two ravens in this ark: my mate and myself. Clearly the Almighty finds me an unclean, unholy species of bird, and He does not want too many of my kind in the world."

Noah shrugged his shoulders. "Very well. But why do you say I too have no liking for you?"

Gazing steadily at him with a baleful eye, the black raven replied, "You wish to send a bird out to fly far and wide, so that it may return and tell you what other regions of the earth look like. You could take one of the 'clean, pure' birds: You have seven pairs of each kind; if anything happens to the one you send out, there will be six pairs left to build nests and raise baby birds. Yet you choose to send me. What if the heat of the sun or the cold of the north is too much for me, and I never come back alive? Then my mate will bear no young ravens, and when my mate dies, not a single one of my kind will be left in the world. Clearly you hate me, for you do not care, and you force me to leave."

Noah laughed. "Why do you think you are so important? What great loss will it be to the world if no ravens are left? Since the Almighty regards you as an unclean, unholy bird, we cannot offer your kind as a sacrifice to Him. And a raven's flesh is no fit food for anyone. Furthermore, why should I treat you with pity and kindness, when ravens do not even take good care of their baby birds? Now that the flood has made the world such a cruel place, it is fitting to send you into it first. Then stop pouting and sulking, and get along with you. . . . Why, just look at you—almost two feet in length. Few birds are so big, strong and husky. Nothing will happen to you. . . . Off you go now; and when you come back, tell me everything you have seen."

With a hoarse malevolent cry, the raven fluttered

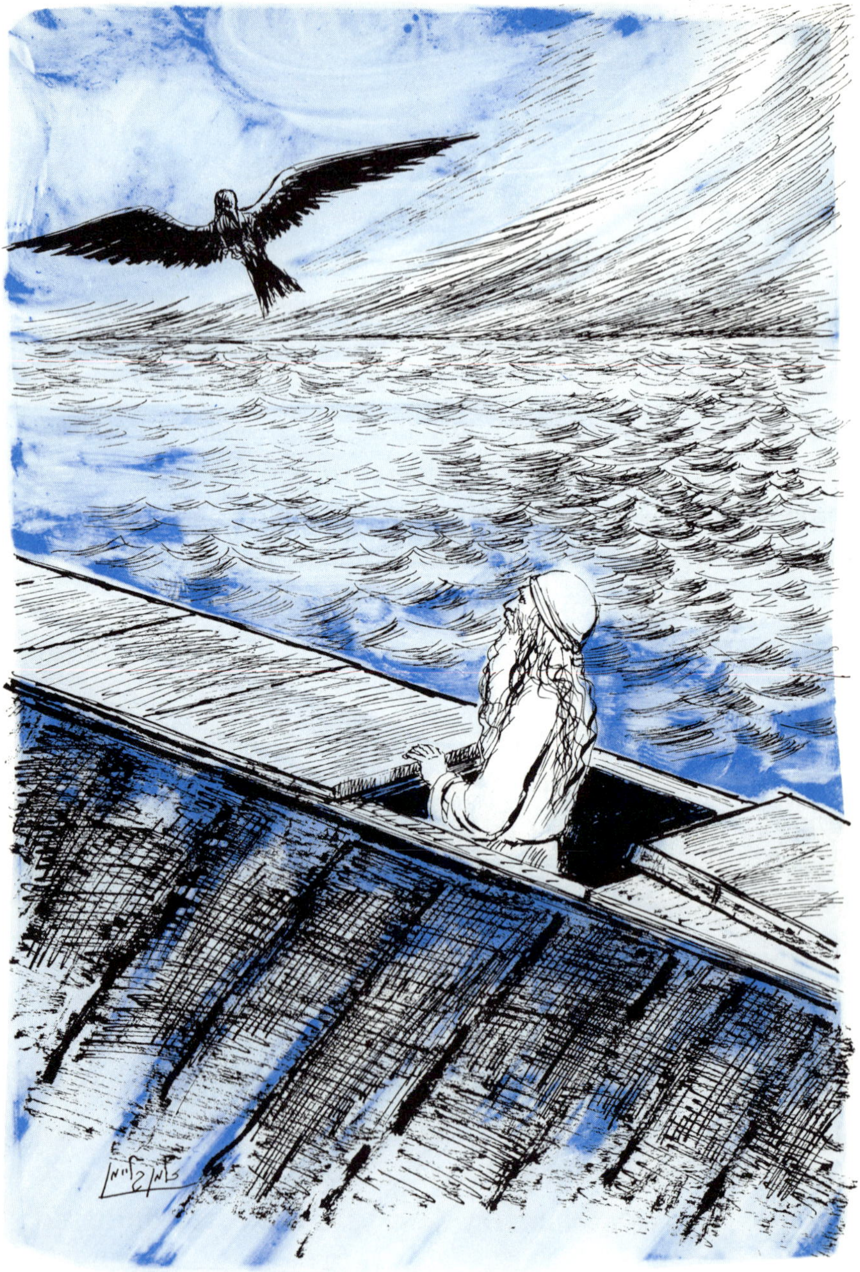

its wings and sailed off into the air between the sky and the water. Noah laughed again, and closed up the opening that served as a window.

But in an hour the raven was back, making an infernal racket as it cried hoarsely and beat with its beak on the wood that blocked up the window. Wearily Noah went and opened the window, and the jet-black raven landed once more on his arm. "Why are you here?" asked Noah.

"Where else is there to go?" the raven retorted. "Have you seen the world outside? No, of course not. You stay here, dry and comfortable, and you send *me* out. Do you want me to drown? There is nothing out there but water—no place to rest, no food to eat. Why do you want me to die and leave my mate a widow at so young an age?"

Noah smiled. He knew the black bird was merely lazy and quarrelsome. It could hardly have flown really far and become very tired in an hour. Vexed and impatient, he was about to send it off again with orders to travel around for at least several hours. But then he heard the words of the Almighty: "Let the creature stay. There *is* a chance that it may come to harm if it flies too far and cannot return before its strength gives out. And the time will come when ravens will be needed in the world."

"When will *that* be?" asked Noah. "When will such an ugly, raucous bird ever be of use to anyone?"

"Well over a thousand years from now," came the Almighty's reply, "a most religious man will arise, named Elijah the prophet. To teach his people that they must worship Me, he will bring a drought upon their land, and no rain will fall. Just as there is too much water now on the earth, so will the farms in his land have no water at all, and nothing will grow there. In their fear and anger, the people will seek to punish that prophet Elijah; but he will flee to hide far from any man—and then only the ravens will bring him food, until he can safely leave."

"Very well," said Noah. "I shall let this ugly creature be lazy and pamper itself in the ark."

In the next few days, whenever he thought the large black bird had rested enough, Noah sent it out again and again—but with no better luck. An hour or two after it flew off, it was back, rapping with its beak and screaming hoarsely to be taken in. Finally Noah spoke sharply to it before he sent it out yet once more: "Go a good long distance this time before you return to tell me how tired you are." The raven glared at him more hatefully than ever, and with a harsh cry it was off.

This time it flew long and steadily, and it found good luck (although for Noah the luck was no good at all). For it reached a tall mountain at last, far from the ark; and strewn about the mountain-top were the bodies of animals which had perished in the flood. Since the creation of the world, ravens had eaten only leaves and vegetables. But the soul of this black crow was as ugly as its looks; and with a shrill cry it pounced on a dead animal and began feeding on the flesh. So it is that since then the raven is called "omnivorous," able to eat both vegetables and meat.

Having eaten its fill, the black ugly bird flew about hoarsely, crying its defiance and scorn of Noah and the ark. At all costs, it would never go back. Here at the mountain it could rest and sleep; there was food enough for it until the flood-water would disappear completely.

As the days went by, Noah realized the raven was gone for good. It was the seventeenth of Tammuz, exactly a week since he had sent out the raven for the first time. With a sigh of relief he took a dove (of which there were seven pairs, since it was a clean, pure species). At least, thought Noah, he would no longer have to deal with a lazy, quarrelsome, hateful bird.

One of the gentlest of all the winged creatures, the dove flew swiftly and silently through the opening that served as a window. Soon it seemed no more than a moving dot against the sky, as Noah watched it disappear in the distance.

Many hours passed before the dove returned; and it pecked ever so gently at the blocked-up window. When Noah opened it and let the little bird in, he had no need to ask anything. If it came back, it had found no dry land in its long flight.

Noah waited a week, and on the twenty-fourth of

Tammuz he sent the dove soaring out again. Once more it flew straight and long, but this time to the country that was to be the homeland of the people of Israel in later centuries. On this land, the holiest part of the world, no rain had fallen directly during the forty days and nights of the flood, and few well-springs had come pouring up from the ground. But as the flood-waters rose everywhere high above the earth, they flowed into this holy land from the neighboring countries, and it too was completely covered by water.

Everywhere else, where the flood had come directly, the crashing, surging, tearing water destroyed every single tree and plant, until nothing remained. In the country that was to become, centuries later, the homeland of Israel, the trees and plants remained, although the water had gathered to a great height above them. Now, as the flood-water gradually disappeared, a little more every day, the tops of a few trees could be seen at last on the hills and mountains of the holy land.

The dove flew on to a place that the people of Israel were to call the Mount of Olives, in a city that would be named Jerusalem. And there it saw the top of an olive tree. To the little bird's eyes it looked as lovely as Paradise. It swooped down to rest a long while on the tree-top. When its heart was no longer beating so fast and its energies had returned, it tore off a single olive leaf with its beak. The leaf firmly in its mouth, it began its long return journey to the ark.

The deepening dark of evening was spreading slowly through the world, as the dove reached the ark. It had no need to rap or call to be let in, for Noah stood at the opened window, anxiously waiting for it. The little bird settled on his arm and was still.

Noah could hardly believe his eyes as he saw the olive leaf, still whole and fresh, in the mouth of the dove. "Somewhere a tree is yet growing after so terrible a flood," he said in wonder, "and at least its topmost part is already above the water. Well, that is good news; and I thank you, my dear dove, for bringing it to me. But I know what you meant by taking this leaf and bringing it. You are a bird, and like every winged creature, more than anything else you fiercely want to be free—free to roam and soar wherever your wings can take you. . . . I can almost hear the words you would say, if you could pray: *O sovereign Ruler of the whole world, let my food be as bitter as this olive leaf, as long as You give it to me from Your hand, letting me find it in the world about. I would rather have that than food sweet as honey, if it must be given me by the hand of a human being while I remain in his power.*"

Did he only imagine it, or was there really a teardrop in the eye of the little bird? "Do not fear, gentle dove," he whispered. "I too pray for the day we can leave the ark, to live freely in the world. And if the top of an olive-tree has already appeared above the flood-water, it cannot be much longer before land appears too. Soon, soon you shall fly away and not return."

Yet another week did Noah wait, until the first of Av (the eleventh month of the Jewish calendar); and for the third time he sent the dove flying off across the water. It was sixty days since the "ocean" that covered the earth had begun to disappear, and by now it was almost gone completely. Much of it had evaporated into the air, and more flowed back into the depths of the earth. Everywhere the tops of hills and mountains could be seen.

Straight as an arrow, the dove returned to the Mount of Olives in the country that was to be the land of Israel some day. Now many trees could be seen there, completely clear of the flood-water, as strong and healthy as ever. With leaves and fruits aplenty for food, the dove remained there, and flew back to the ark no more.

12

RETURN TO LAND

The days and the weeks passed slowly by, as life continued unchanged in the ark. Two months after the dove had left, on the first of Tishri, Noah went once more to open the window. And he smiled. For at last, far below the mountain peaks of Ararat, on which the ark stood, he could see land. Then he caught his breath. Off in the distance, somewhere between heaven and earth, he saw dazzling rays of silver and gold. At some point the sun's blazing light was finally piercing the gloomy layers of cloud. Amid the chill cold that made him ache, it was a sight that warmed his heart.

Noah wondered: Now that the flood-waters were gone, could they leave the ark? He went to the lowest deck and tried the door. But the door would not budge. There was no lock of any kind on it, since the Almighty had not told him to make any. Once all the creatures that belonged in the ark were safely inside, the Almighty Himself had sealed the door shut, and no force on earth could open it. Now it was still shut, sealed up as firmly as ever.

Noah felt angry: Why must they all stay on in the ark, if the flood-water was completely gone? He thought of calling his three young, strong sons to break the door down. *No,* he decided: the Almighty must have a good reason for keeping it shut. The ground must be loose watery mud everywhere, and any man or beast that tried to walk on it would sink deep down. He would have to wait patiently for the door to open of itself. Meanwhile he would have to continue feeding the animals by day and by night, finding time only for short naps, never sleeping or resting properly.

Noah groaned. The constant, endless work in the ark had ruined his health, leaving him chilled and aching with tiredness all over. He could not bear it much longer. "O Lord," he whispered, "sovereign Ruler of land and water and all that lives on them, I pray You: take me out of this ark in which You put me, for it has become a prison to my spirit, and I am so deeply wearied and ailing."

In the silence of endless sky and land, Noah heard a voice like an echo: "Very soon you will leave—when one year will be ended since you entered the ark."

It took seven weeks for the deep mud on the ground to dry. As time is reckoned by the movement of the earth around the sun, it was exactly one year after the flood had begun. And in the side of the ark, the great door swung open. In the sky the sun blazed again in all its glory, for the heavy covering of cloud had vanished at last, swept away by wintry winds.

Once more the world was as it had always been since creation, as though the great flood had never come. But traces of the flood remained. Gone from the earth was the rich fertile topsoil, in which grains, fruits and vegetables had grown so easily, so rapidly, so splendidly. In the country that was to be the Land of Israel, there remained three well-springs which had opened up during the flood. They were to prove for all time that the enormous flood had really come upon the world, so that no one could claim it had never happened. To this day (it is said) one of those three provides the hot water in the mineral springs of Tiberias, that bring healing to the sick.

In the ark the excitement was powerful indeed. Through the window and the door the creatures could see the dry ground in the radiant sunshine. With a thousand voices and sounds the animals told one another the happy news that very soon they could leave this floating home which had imprisoned them while it kept them safe. They stirred and moved restlessly, with a new desire to roam again in the dark woods and green pastures, in the valleys and mountains and jungle-lands. Birds which had been still for months now preened and stretched their wings, and sang once more their lovely trills and calls, knowing they would soon fly away free to their heart's content.

The door was wide open; and before it the ground was high enough so that there was no need to jump down. Yet Noah stood inside, waiting; and every creature there waited with him; for in the ark he was master, and none dared leave before him.

"Father, why do you wait?" asked his son Shem. "Come," said Japheth, "let us be going."

"No!" he retorted. "We entered by the Almighty's command, and we shall leave only at His command."

At that moment the words of the Almighty came to him: "Come out of the ark, you and your wife, and your sons and your sons' wives with you" (Genesis 8:16). Noah motioned to his family to make ready to leave with him. "Bring out with you," the words of the Almighty continued, "every living being that you have there, of every kind of creature—birds and beasts and every crawling thing that creeps on the earth; and let them breed their young in large numbers upon the earth, to multiply and increase upon the earth" (Genesis 8:17).

Noah stepped forward. Yet even as his foot touched the threshold, he stopped and moved no further. For suddenly he thought, "What is the use of going out? My family and I are the only people left on earth. In time we will have grandchildren and great-grandchildren, until we form many tribes and nations. What if the Almighty should decide some day that my descendants are evil? He will bring another flood upon the world, to destroy them too. We might as well stay here until we all die and no human beings are left on earth. Why raise families if they can be wiped out at any moment?" And he remained where he was.

"Noah," whispered a heavenly voice, "why do you stay?"

"O mighty Ruler of the world," said he, "will You bring any more floods to cover all the earth?"

"You have My word," replied the voice. "Upon My oath, there will be no more floods to destroy the entire earth." Only then did Noah step out.

His sons were about to follow him, when a tremendous roar made them stop where they were. In all the past months in the ark, the lion had suffered from a mild fever, which made it lie tame and quiet. Now that it was time to leave, the fever suddenly left it, and all at once the king of the animals realized how it been kept a prisoner of a sort for a full year. Deeply angered, the majestic beast gave its mighty roar and leaped out ahead of everyone. Blaming Noah for its "imprisonment," the wild creature bit him in the hip, and fled.

As Noah cried out in pain, his wife and sons carried him to smooth flat ground, where they treated the wound as best they could. From the ark's upper deck they brought special herbs (where they had stored them yet before the flood); and these stopped the bleeding and eased the deep pain, letting the wound heal rapidly.

Noah was glad to lie quietly and rest in the warming sun, happy that the cold gruelling year was over.

Never had the blue of the sky looked so lovely to him.

Meanwhile, his three sons and their wives got all the animals out of the ark in good order. The creatures too were glad to feel the sun, and solid ground at last under their feet. Happily they leapt and frolicked, and shook themselves. Then they ran off their separate ways with joyous cries and roars, back into the world they knew.

At last the air was still. Of the many thousands of creatures, none were left except the fowl and domestic animals that would stay with the human beings.

Noah sat up and looked about. The ground under him was nothing but hard caked mud. No crops of food could grow in it until light rain softened it a little. And even then the soil would be poor: it would never grow the same wonderful grain, fruits and vegetables as before the flood.

Suddenly Noah felt how very strange the world was all about him. Except for his own family, not a soul was to be seen anywhere. In all the years of his life there had always been neighbors, people he knew, passing by to greet him and chat a while. Now there was no one at all. For the first time Noah understood how cruel the flood had been. Tears came to his eyes.

"O mighty Ruler of the world," he cried, "You are called the Merciful One. You should have had mercy on Your living beings."

The reply came: "Do you say this to Me now? When I told you to make an ark because I would bring the flood to destroy every living being, why did you not ask Me *then* to have mercy? Then it was enough for you to know that you and your family would be safe. Once you saw that the people in the world about you would not listen to your warnings, you built your ark, and you gave them never another thought. Now, when the destruction is over, you ask Me for mercy!"

Noah realized how wrong he was. He had indeed spoken foolishly; and truly he should have prayed for mercy before the flood came. He wanted to do something now to make the Almighty forgive him. And more—he wanted to show the Almighty how deeply thankful he was that his family and he *were* alive and safe after this dreadful year.

As people always did in those early centuries when the world was young, Noah decided to offer sacrifices. His sons gathered large stones, and with these he built an altar. But he could not make the offering himself, for the lion had injured him too severely when it went tearing out of the ark. Though the wound healed soon, he remained lame for the rest of his life; and a man with a defect in his body was not fit to offer up sacrifices.

When they were young, Noah's three sons had studied with his grandfather Methuselah, to learn from him the great wisdom of Enoch. Of the three, Shem had learned it best of all, to know the wishes and the ways of the Almighty. So it was that Noah now asked Shem, his wise and religious son, to offer the sacrifices for him. From the ark they brought a special set of garments that Noah had saved. They were holy garments, which Adam had made long ago, to wear only when he stood at an altar to bring offerings. Adam had given them to Seth, and Seth to his son; and so they came down from father to son, until Methuselah gave them to Noah. Now he handed them to Shem.

"Put them on," said Noah, "for you shall go to the altar in my place. And from this day on, these holy garments shall be yours; for you alone of my children are fit to offer sacrifices."

They chose an ox and a sheep, two turtle-doves, and a pair of pigeons. (Since these were creatures which the Almighty considered pure and clean, they had kept seven pairs of each in the ark.) And it is told that the Almighty was pleased that the people who remained on earth did not stupidly turn to foolish idol-worship, but rather chose to worship Him, to thank Him for being alive and to win His favor. He was especially pleased to see Shem before Him in religious devotion; some day, He knew, a descendant of Shem named Abraham would come into the world.

So it was that the Almighty blessed Noah and his sons: "Increase and multiply to raise large families, and fill the earth. All the beasts of the earth and birds of the air, all that creep on the ground, and the entire fish of the sea, shall go in fear and dread of you: they shall be in your power. Every living, moving creature is yours to use for food from now on; I give you everything to use, like the green vegetables of the field . . ." (Genesis 9:1-3). Until the flood, human beings ate only the food that grew in their fields, out of the earth. From that time on, they were to eat meat also—the food that came from the flesh of birds, beasts and fish. Thus people would have the right to end the life of creatures which they needed for food. So some might think they had the right to kill people too, if they wanted to. But the Almighty now gave a strict law: "Whoever sheds a man's blood, *his* blood will be shed by man; for in the image of God did He make man" (Genesis 9:6). Every human being is a wonderful, precious creation, a little like the Almighty Himself; and no one has the right to kill another person, whatever his reasons. Whoever commits a murder, in one way or another he will pay for it with his own life, even if no policeman catches him and no judge sentences him. Fate itself will overtake him—for it is the Almighty's law, that He now told to Noah.

There was one more thing that the Creator of the world told Noah and his sons: "Now I make a covenant, a solemn agreement, with you and your descendants after you, and with every living creature that was with you—birds, beasts of burden, and every animal of the earth. . . . I shall keep this covenant with you all: that never more shall all living creatures of flesh be destroyed by the waters of a flood; never again shall there be a flood to devastate the earth" (Genesis 9:9-11).

In the silence that lay about them like a cloak, Noah and his sons listened on, as the Almighty's words continued: "Look up in the distance." Far off in the sky above them, a faint mist shimmered between heaven and earth, like a delicate gossamer veil. And as the sun's splendid rays played on it and streamed through it, the mist became a glowing rainbow, sparkling, glistening with every radiant color that the human eye can know. Never before, since the creation of the world, had a rainbow appeared. Never before had Noah and his family seen anything so utterly lovely.

Once more they heard the Almighty's words: "This is the sign of the covenant, the solemn agreement I make between Me and you and every living creature with you, for all generations: I have set My rainbow in the cloud . . . Whenever I form clouds over the earth, in the clouds the rainbow shall appear; and even if you do not see it, it will make Me remember My covenant that is between Me and you and every living creature of flesh—and never shall the waters rise in flood again, to destroy all that lives. There, in the clouds, the rainbow will be—glistening radiantly when the sun shines after a downpour—and as I look on it, I will remember this everlasting covenant between God and every living creature that dwells on earth . . ." (Genesis 9:12-16).

A great peace and calm settled in their hearts.

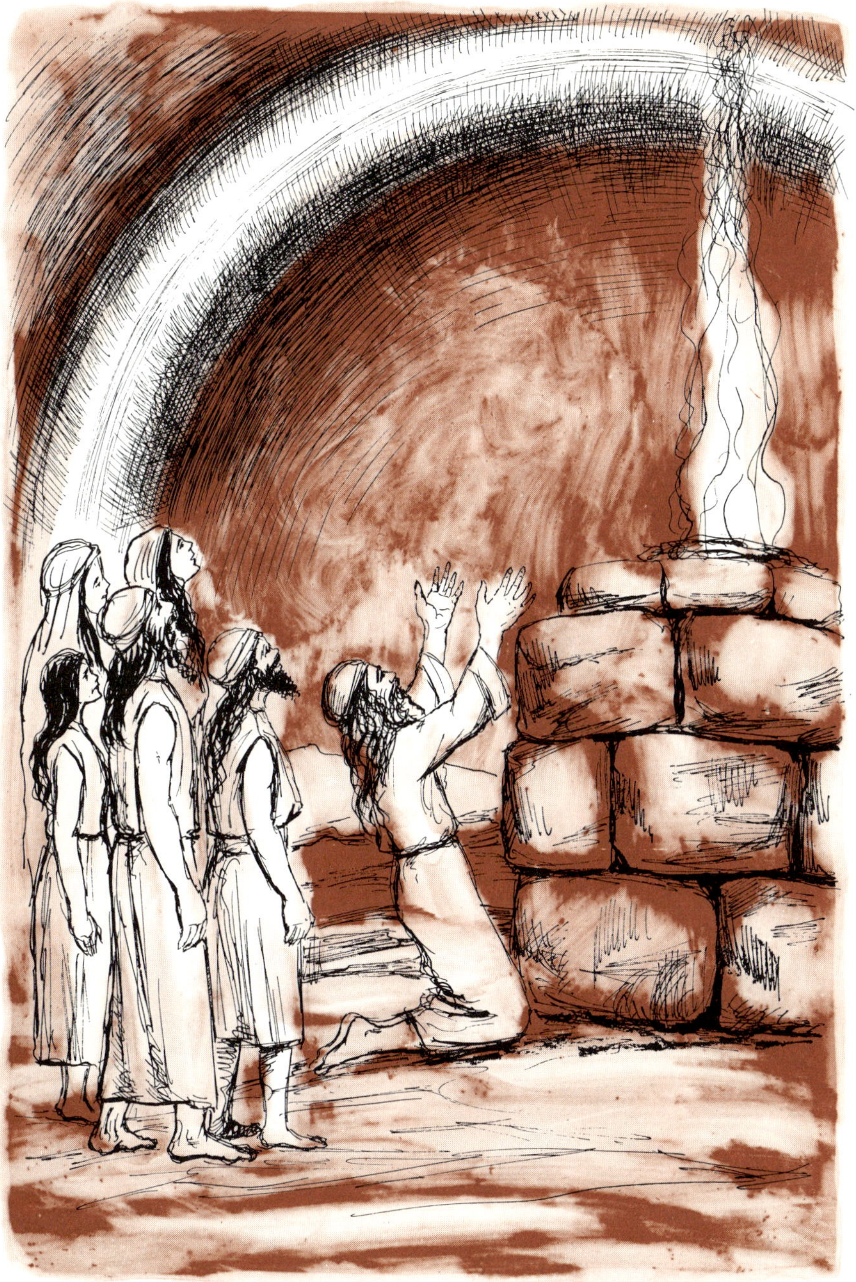

Again and again the Almighty's words had mentioned the covenant. After such a repeated promise that was really a vow, they and their descendants would never have to wonder and fear whether such a terrible disaster could happen again. Till the end of time, mankind could be sure that no matter how badly people sinned, life on earth would never be entirely wiped out.

The lovely shimmering rainbow brought a song to their hearts, as Noah and his sons set about building new homes for themselves and their womenfolk. Human life on earth would go on with them, free of the evil that once filled the world.